Emilio's mastery of his craft shines thru again!

This book grabs leadership lessons from our history so that we can control our destiny! His articulate appreciation of what is required of us before we get to the ballot box makes this book indispensable!

Vipp Jaswal, Head International Affairs, Fox News Channel

"Who would you rather have a beer with?"

For election after election, the presidential candidate Americans polled said they would prefer to share a beer with has become President of the United States. Perhaps this isn't the best criteria for electing "the leader of the free world".

Brilliantly written and highly accessible, Emilio Iodice's "Selecting a President: The Most Important Decision YOU Will Make in 2016" precisely delineates what American voters should be looking for in their leader.

With an enlightened historical perspective, Professor Iodice provides a forward looking treatise of the qualities and characteristics an informed electorate should be seeking out to base their decision on which candidate would best serve the country in 2016.

The stakes are high in the upcoming election. "Selecting a President" elevates the discussion in a correspondingly high fashion. It is a must read for anyone desirous of electing the most qualified and capable person to be the next President of the United States.

Emilio Iodice provides an exhaustive historical accounting of the challenges – both global and national in content and scope – faced by American presidents since George Washington. Complemented by visual images and pertinent quotes, Iodice examines that salient characteristics of what the Office of the Presidency commands: moral fortitude and emotional intelligence; reform-mindedness and ongoing connectivity to constituents; the ability to synthesize opinions and facts in the decision-making process; upstanding personal character – both on and off the stage; accountability and reliability; commitment to effecting greater civil rights through expanded access to educational, housing, and vocational opportunities; and diplomatic adeptness in a world of constant conflict. As this iteration ostensibly represents a tall order for the candidate, understanding that the position reflects a beacon of hope and posits an example of courage to the entire world, these characteristics must be apparent in the individual chosen for the highest office in the land.

Iodice also emphasizes that this position is even more complex and exacting in the present age as communication channels are ever-present. Furthermore, global and domestic issues are more pressing now more than ever and the candidate must come to the table with a firm understanding and willingness to tackle matters of climate change, immigration, campaign finance reform, race relations, gun control, the growing disparity of income and the gentrification of society, the equal treatment of all people, crumbling infrastructure, the need for meaningful employment and educational opportunities, shifting foreign policy with nuclear annihilation ever present, increasing population growth and growing resource scarcity, and incarceration, law enforcement, and universal healthcare deficits.

Whereas the US has historically been viewed as "the greatest country on earth," the statistics regarding its poverty, life expectancy, and infant mortality rates; educational attainment (particularly in Math and

Science), access to comprehensive healthcare services; increasing destruction of entire regions by accentuated weather-related events; collapse of unions and collective bargaining; and continued inequality of pay provide a divergence. In this light, choosing from the 2016 presidential candidates will exact a heavy analysis of performance capabilities. To aid this process, Iodice provides a comprehensive checklist of requisite qualities to assist the voter in discerning actual facts in an era of uncertainty, ignorance, and fear-mongering, inflammatory talking points.

There truly is nothing more important to democracy as a well-informed electorate. And, as he appropriately summarizes the 2016 presidential race, "The Stakes Are Planetary!"

"An eye for an eye makes the whole world blind." - Mahatma Gandhi
"Education is the most powerful weapon which you can use to change the world."
— **Nelson Mandela**

Elizabeth F. R. Gingerich, J.D.
Editor-in-Chief, *Journal of Values-Based Leadership*
The Louis S. and Mary L. Morgal Chair of Christian Business Ethics
Valparaiso University, Valparaiso, IN USA

Emilio Iodice

2016
Selecting The President

THE MOST IMPORTANT DECISION
YOU WILL MAKE IN 2016

WHAT <u>YOU</u> MUST LOOK FOR

LEADERSHIP QUALITIES THE PRESIDENT <u>MUST HAVE</u>

ISSUES THE NEW ADMINISTRATION WILL FACE

NO ONE SHOULD VOTE FOR PRESIDENT BEFORE READING THIS BOOK <u>FIRST</u>

<u>A SPECIAL CHECKLIST FOR VOTERS</u>

The Oval Office, Courtesy White House Museum http://www.whitehousemuseum.org/index.htm

Copyright Emilio Iodice 2015 all rights reserved No. 1-2795555391

Dedicated to those I love and those who love me, in particular my grandchildren, Sofia, Helena, Lukas and Anna.

ALSO BY EMILIO IODICE

Profiles in Leadership from Caesar to Modern Times

A Kid from Philadelphia, Mario Lanza, the Voice of the Poets

Sisters

Future Shock 2.0, The Dragon Brief, a thriller about 2020 of fiction based on fact.

Reflections: Stories of Love, Inspiration, Remembrance and Power

Acknowledgements

In any task there are those who inspire and there are those who assist and there are those who do both. The people I would like to thank for helping me in preparing this book have done both with their help and with their inspiration. Each has told me of the urgency of preparing a book that reflects on the qualities that we need to make an informed and intelligent decision on who should be the President of the United States.

Vipp Jaswal of Fox News came up with the idea. At the end of a radio interview that Vipp brilliantly conducted with me, he said that a book was needed that portrayed the leadership qualities of what we require in a President and to base it on history. That is the mission of this book. It is designed to be *timeless* and to be used for this election and every election from now on. I would like to thank another Radio Talk Show Host, Glenn Klein of Magnum Media. Glenn asked interesting and provocative questions during my interview with him that showed me that this work was essential for all of us to select our next Commander in Chief. Professor Elizabeth Gingrich of Valparaiso University in Indiana has been someone who I admire and respect for her great professionalism. In addition to be a splendid educator, Elizabeth is the Editor of a journal I have contributed too: The Journal of Values Based Leadership. I asked her to comment on the book because of the how much I value her thoughts about leadership and Presidential leadership in particular.

I owe a special debt of gratitude to Dr. Ronald White of the Huntington Library. He is one of the foremost experts on Abraham Lincoln. I have learned more from his work about our sixteenth President than anyone else. He inspired me by his work to move vigorously to prepare this book and to make it a scholarly publication that was heavily researched like the amazing books he has published. Thanks to him, we know that Abraham Lincoln still matters and remains a model that all leaders should emulate.

I thank Claudio Minenza who worked hard to finish the final, camera ready document to submit to my publisher. He was amazing in providing timely and accurate page by page preparation of the complete manuscript and demonstrated what a great professional can do in a very short time.

A person who has done so much with so little is the one who has shaped this book into a work that looks and is professional and enjoyable to read. Emily Moss is a sterling professional who specializes in graphic design but she does so much more. She took a draft filled with words, images, ideas, quotes and references and put it in a form that anyone can relate to whether it is an eBook or paperback or hard cover. She made the book be what it should be: A valuable and timeless tool for all to help us make the most important decision we will ever make: Selecting the President of the United States.

Thank you again to one and all.

Emilio Iodice

Table of Contents

Emilio Iodice

2016 Selecting the President

Preface

In the midst of the boisterous 2016 presidential campaign comes a smart and entertaining book by Emilio Iodice. An accomplished author who has served both as an administrator of a major university and a senior American diplomat, Iodice invites his readers into an illuminating journey into *Selecting A President.* As a presidential biographer, I appreciate his selection of the key leadership qualities you and I should look for in choosing our next president.

Readers will enjoy Iodice's fast-paced narrative style. A leader himself, standing now for years with one foot in Europe and the other in the United States, he employs a wide angle political lens. Iodice anchors his examination of leadership qualities in insightful analyses of these attributes in American presidents, including George Washington, Thomas Jefferson, Abraham Lincoln, Franklin Delano Roosevelt, John F. Kennedy, Ronald Reagan, and Bill Clinton.

I especially enjoyed his chapter on "Emotional Intelligence." Beginning with a thoughtful appraisal of Abraham Lincoln, he examines the role that self-awareness, self-regulation, and empathy played in what many of us would esteem our greatest president. Sadly, these qualities seem in short supply in too many running for political office today. I call Lincoln our most "eloquent" president, but Iodice allows us to see that beneath Lincoln's gift for public speaking was his equal gift for public listening.

Another dimensions of this timely book that will win it a wide audience is Iodice's artistic use of photographs and political cartoons. The saying is correct that "a picture is worth a thousand words." In my new biography of Ulysses S.Grant I have discovered the power to political cartoons which Iodice employs

I enthusiastically commend *Selecting A President*. A wise and winsome author has given to us a trustworthy companion as we chart our own path as citizens in the campaign year 2016.

Ronald C. White, Jr., is the author of A. Lincoln: *A Biography*

Foreword

When I was a boy I was told that anybody could become President. Now I'm beginning to believe it. Clarence Darrow

Dear Reader:

This book is an **urgent wakeup call**! We are facing a critical Presidential election. It is happening during one of the most dangerous periods in world history and American history. We are confronting decisions about our wellbeing and those who inhabit our planet. *__We cannot make a mistake.__*

I wrote this for you, your families, your children and their children. It is a tool to make us think and choose intelligently. The selection of President of the United States is the most important political judgement any people can make. *__It is reserved for the citizens of the US.__*

How can we formulate a rational choice? *__Any decision should be based on facts before we inject feelings.__* Emotion and "gut feel" are important but not enough. They help determine if a candidate *__appears__* to have the qualities we feel are essential to guide us through the uncharted waters of the nuclear age, the internet age and the age of the global village where we are all intertwined to survive and thrive on this small, "blue dot" in the universe. In addition to emotion, we need truth, reality, and evidence to help us make our choice. This is where history comes in. This is where we define what we need. This is where *__We the people__* are the ones who should set the stage, direct the players and make the choices. We should tell the "establishment" what *__WE__* want.

This book delves into historic examples of Presidents who exhibited the qualities I believe we need today. I based my list of leadership traits on four decades of personal research and studying Presidential leadership and all its components. I used this knowledge to create my choices. Now I present it to you with examples of Presidents in action. Their judgments were based on their qualities. As they acted, they revealed to us who they were. They showed the *"right stuff"* to lead and craft decisions. Some of those choices we still live with today. I also used the wisdom and findings of scholars who dedicated lifetimes to uncovering and separating facts from fiction. As you can see, I utilized their insights to help us understand clearly what abilities our Presidents had and how they used that talent to lead. I have referenced them throughout the text to back up my reasoning. The book is filled with quotes. They help amplify and round out our insights and reflection on each chapter and section.

Use this tool as a compass, a guide and a way to think through your determination whether it is in a Presidential primary or in the general election.

Remember, we as Americans have a great obligation to ourselves and the world. The responsibility to select the President of the United States of America is ours and ours alone. Let us make it wisely and confidently. Let us make it together as a free people who love liberty and all it means for us and those who look to us as the lighthouse in a world filled with darkness.

Emilio Iodice

Introduction: A Book for Voters

The Desk of the President of the United States, termed the "Resolute Desk." Courtesy Jimmy Carter Library and Museum

This book is a <u>Tool for Voters</u>. It is designed to help us intelligently sort through *the confusion* of who to select as a candidate of our Party and who to select as President, especially when no two candidates are alike.

Who will *WE* Choose to Sit at the Resolute Desk?

This is by far the most significant decision we make in our lifetime. We are voting for the most important office on the planet. We cannot make a mistake yet many times we do. We often choose in a climate of uncertainty and ignorance. We must select carefully who should sit at the <u>Resolute Desk</u> in the Oval Office.

We listen to commentators and politicians and their proxies. We talk to friends and family and then we make our *prediction*. Our vote is a *forecast* about the future. In reality, selecting the President of the

United States is a matter of life or death, success or failure, peace or war, poverty or prosperity. We need to minimize the risk by making it ***intelligently*** and with as much information as possible about ***who we want in the job and the qualities we should insist upon.***

If one asks, what is the one quality above all that the President of the United States must have, it is by far, **Character.** What do we mean by character? It includes **integrity, honesty, truthfulness and a moral compass.** It predicts behavior. If we assume the candidate is experienced, communicates well, has presence, charisma, emotional intelligence and confidence, than the overriding quality to look for is character. **As we shall demonstrate in this book, character and other traits are essential for us to trust the nuclear button and our lives, our sacred fortunes and those of the people of the world to the person who will sit at the Resolute Desk.**

The Presidency is more than an American institution. It is the focus of feelings for the people. It is more important than the Congress or the Supreme Courts because it is the easiest office the public can identify with. The President is a symbolic leader who holds the hopes and dreams of the people in his or her hands. It is the closest we get to an American monarch, a planetary monarch.

This book is a guide. It is about what we should look for in terms of the 2016 Presidential election and **what we should *always look for*** in the leadership attributes that ***WE*** should demand from a President. Our work is based on examples of some of strongest and weakest Chief Executives. Some were imminently successful. They had nearly all the traits we need. We should look to them as models as we choose our President in 2016 and from now on.

The last chapter has a **VOTERS CHECKLIST, LEADERSHIP QUALITIES AND THE CANDIDATES.** This is a tool to help us draw conclusions about each contender for the White House, first in the primaries and then in the general election. It includes web sites for the latest comparisons of each candidate on the key issues facing us and where they stand. With this data, the Checklist and what we know from this book we should be able to make an intelligent decision on who to vote for in 2016.

The Earth and the Moon, Courtesy NASA

We need to remember that we are electing a **planetary leader** who is the most powerful leader in the world.

Part One: 2016

Chapter One: Presidential Power

Every four years we elect a new Chief Executive. The person chosen is not just President of the United States. The position is of global leader, global decision maker and global visionary. It is a responsibility that requires us to reflect on the qualities we want and need in our nation's new Commander in Chief. The power to choose is in our hands. We must take it seriously and understand the implications. Failure is not an option.

The Global Leader

Article II of the U.S. Constitution vests the executive power of the United States in the President who is the Supreme Commander of American military forces around the world and often referred to as the Commander in Chief. In addition, the President has other essential responsibilities.

The Roles of the President of the United States

What are the roles of the President? The person selected must fulfill a number of complex and interconnected functions:[1]

Chief of State: The President as the Ceremonial Head of the US.

---

[1] Pearson, The President's Job Description,
http://assets.pearsonschool.com/asset_mgr/legacy/200938/section1_jobdescription_26523_1.pdf

Chief Executive: The President as the holder of the executive power of the United States.

Chief Administrator: The President as the leader of the Executive branch of the Federal Government

Chief Diplomat: The President as the main architect of American Foreign Policy and the nation's Chief Spokesperson to other countries.

Commander in Chief: The top person in charge of the nation's armed forces.

Chief Legislator: The President as the main author of public policy.

Chief of Party: The President as the leader of his or her political party.

Andrew Jackson considered himself a forceful President who used all his powers. 1832 political cartoon, Courtesy Library of Congress

In "The Presidential Difference," Fred I. Greenstein explained the role today:

The power of modern American presidents manifests itself in its purest form in the global arena, where their actions as commander in chief can determine the fate of the human race. This was most strikingly evident in the extended nuclear standoff between the United States and the Soviet Union that followed World War II. However, the president's latitude for independent action is even greater in the unstructured post-cold war world than it was during the cold war, when the threat of mutual destruction concentrated minds and constrained actions.

Presidential power is less potentially apocalyptic at home than abroad, but the occupant of the Oval Office is also of critical domestic importance. The power to nullify legislation gives the chief executive the capacity to thwart the will of Congress, unless his veto is overridden by two-thirds of the Senate and House of Representatives. [2]

The President has power of budget allocations and the execution of laws. He or she can sway public opinion and, even when facing impeachment, still retain their formal powers.

All of this would lead one to expect the qualities that bear on a president's leadership to be subjected to the closest possible attention. That is far from the case. To be sure, every president has been the object of a deluge of prose, first during his presidency, then in the memoirs of his associates, and later in studies based on the declassified records of his administration. Yet, much of that outpouring is directed to the ends the president sought rather than the means he used to advance them, and a large portion of it bears on the merits of his policies rather than the attributes that shaped his leadership. [3]

1. Fred I. Greenstein, The Presidential Difference, Leadership Style From FDR to Clinton Free Press, NY, NY 2000, Chapter 1.
2. Greenstein, page 2

President Roosevelt was accused of trying to "pack" the Supreme Court and add new members when the Court voted New Deal laws unconstitutional, February 8, 1937, Courtesy *Chicago News*, "What Did Uncle Vote For?"

The system of "checks and balances" was set up by the founders of the American republic as part of the US Constitution to specify the functions and responsibilities of the President, the Congress and the Supreme Court and to maintain a balance of power and "check" and limit each branch from becoming too influential. Since the beginning of the United States, the Presidency has evolved and more powers have been given to the President especially in the realm of global affairs.

As a result, it is not enough to select someone with qualities that fit our national needs when the stakes are planetary. The future of the world depends on an America which is strong, just and fair. This is embodied in our history, traditions and institutions and in the Presidency. When we have failed to provide strength, integrity and champion social justice, the world has failed with us. We are the example of democracy, pluralism and impartiality.

Whether we like it or not, people and nations look to America to provide a model of what we all should be. They imitate our culture, examine and study our laws and emulate our ideas and ideals. As a result, we are a lighthouse in the darkness for millions who live beyond our shores. It is a responsibility. We should not shrink from it. We should embrace the task even if we are not without flaws. There is no one else on earth to offer the proper vision and leadership for our globe but the United States of America.

We have no choice. If we fail, the domestic and international forces of intolerance and tyranny will prevail. Our survival is at stake. It is also at risk for those who look to us for leadership across the globe. Since this is the case, we should do all we can to do our part with wisdom, understanding and strength. We have a duty to provide the best leadership possible to a world that is seeking direction based on the principles represented in the American Bill of Rights.

We are not perfect but should strive for perfection. Our leaders are not saints but should seek to be models of integrity. They should be expected to do the right thing even if it is not the right time. We will never solve all our problems but should work to overcome them in good faith and honesty. This will not always be the case, but with proper leadership we can try to resolve the great issues that affect our lives, and the earth we inhabit, with fairness, liberty, justice and reason. The American Presidency symbolizes these principles.

This book is not an endorsement of one candidate over another. It does not dwell on the last three administrations since historians are still judging them. **It is a look at Presidents of the past and what they teach us about what we need today and tomorrow. In actuality, *this book is timeless*. It pertains to this Presidential election and can pertain to any election from now on. It is an ageless tool to help us choose intelligently and rationally based on historic facts.**

Our work is about the characteristics we should demand that the President of the United States have to be the leader of a world that endeavors to provide opportunities for all in an atmosphere of freedom. No one person will have them all. Regardless, we should try to select someone who comes as close to the ideal without the illusion that saints sit in the Oval Office. They do not. At the same time, we cannot tolerate habitual sinners controlling the apparatus of the most powerful country on the planet.

We Elect a Government when we Elect a President

We should realize that we do not elect a President but elect a government. The Chief Executive of America appoints thousands who administer the apparatus of the largest bureaucracy on earth. Those appointees should reflect the same leadership qualities of those who appointed them to roles of public trust. The process of voicing the qualities we need should be from "the bottom up" and not "the top down." By this we mean that we the people should express ourselves as to what we believe best represents our needs, our ideals and our model for leadership.

Select and not settle for the Next President

Courtesy of Pat Oliphant, June 15, 2004, Universal/Uclick[4]

Often times, we are given choices from the political establishment and told what we require in a President. Today we have the communication means to articulate what we feel are the traits that our top leader should have.

We are all connected. Social media provides a new platform for all groups and individuals to communicate, debate, convey and vent feelings from the bottom so that the top understands what we need at

---

[4] The Atlantic, Legendary Cartoonist Pat Oliphant, 'We Are in a Forest of Ignorance.'
http://www.theatlantic.com/politics/archive/2014/09/legendary-cartoonist-pat-oliphant-we-are-in-a-forest-fire-of-ignorance/379524/

this time in our history. **We need to vote in a smarter and more intelligent way for the most important position in our land.**

We should encourage discussion from the classroom to the community to the talk shows and all forms of media until it is clear that we will select and not settle for anyone but the best and brightest to be President of the United States.

Chapter Two: The 2016 Race: What to Look For?

The President is merely the most important among a large number of public servants. He should be supported or opposed exactly to the degree which is warranted by his good conduct or bad conduct, his efficiency or inefficiency in rendering loyal, able, and disinterested service to the Nation as a whole. Therefore it is absolutely necessary that there should be full liberty to tell the truth about his acts, and this means that it is exactly necessary to blame him when he does wrong as to praise him when he does right. Any other attitude in an American citizen is both base and servile. To announce that there must be no criticism of the president, or that we are to stand by the president, right or wrong, is not only unpatriotic and servile, but is morally treasonable to the American public. Nothing but the truth should be spoken about him or anyone else. But it is even more important to tell the truth, pleasant or unpleasant, about him than about anyone else.
Theodore Roosevelt

In addition to the qualifications we will discuss, there are some general factors we should look for in the candidates in primaries:

How they react under stress.

How they plan to tackle the big issues.

How they conduct themselves on and off the campaign.

Personal Presence

In particular, we should watch closely *what they have said and what they say.*

All of these define them as people and as leaders.

Past and Present words and actions matter.

They catch up with a candidate. They are like torpedoes and dynamite if not handled properly. They can sink a nominee or explode when least expected. Often times, words exhibit how candidates think and how they make decisions. Words and phrases carefully constructed and used can become noteworthy. They can either boost chances for success or contribute too or assure defeat.

Their behavior in and out of the Oval Office matters.

The San Francisco Chronical illustrated some of the most famous campaign gaffes in modern presidential contests in a in a September 18th 2012 article by Richard Durham entitled: *Top Ten Campaign Gaffes in Modern Presidential History.*[5]

The examples include the 2004 race between Senator John Kerry and President George W. Bush. Kerry was attacked for changing his mind on a funding bill. "I actually did vote for the $87 billion, before I voted against it," he explained. The sentence was used by his opponents to define him as a "flip flopper" in the minds of voters and may have contributed to his defeat.

---

[5] Richard Durham, Top Ten Campaign Gaffes in Modern Presidential History, September 18th, 2012 San Francisco Chronical (http://blog.sfgate.com/nov05election/2012/09/18/top-ten-campaign-gaffes-in-modern-presidential-history/)

Senator George McGovern and Senator Thomas Eagleton, Courtesy Senate of the United States

Senator George McGovern in the 1972 race to unseat President Richard Nixon had to confront a serious issue. His running mate, vice presidential nominee Tom Eagleton, had suffered from depression and consequently underwent electric shock therapy. Some top Democrats called for Eagleton to be replaced. McGovern was steadfast in his support. "I am one thousand percent for Tom Eagleton and I have no intention of dropping him from the ticket," he insisted. Shortly thereafter, McGovern dropped Eagleton as his running mate. His credibility plummeted. He lost to Nixon in an historic landslide.

In 1976, President Gerald Ford mistakenly stated that Poland was free from the domination of the Soviet Union. It was not. The error haunted Ford throughout the campaign and hurt him with blue collar workers who had families in Eastern Europe. He lost the election to Governor Jimmy Carter of Georgia.

Former Vermont Governor Howard Dean, Courtesy Dean for America

During the race for the Democratic nomination for President in 2004, Howard Dean, the one-time front runner, lost the Iowa caucuses.

By Parker, Courtesy Florida Today, 2004

In his statement conceding defeat, Dean listed states he had targeted for victory and yelled "Yee-haw." Dean's "Scream" became the key story of the night and helped end his chances for the Presidency.

Senator Obama, during the 2008 Presidential race, attempted to explain the frustrations of blue collar workers during a fund raiser with wealthy Democrats in San Francisco by saying:

"And it's not surprising then they get bitter, they cling to guns or religion or antipathy to people who aren't like them or anti-immigrant sentiment or anti-trade sentiment as a way to explain their frustrations."

As President, Obama was often criticized for the comment.

President Lyndon Johnson and Senator Barry Goldwater Courtesy Library of Congress

The 1964 race between President Lyndon Johnson and Senator Barry Goldwater was a test between conservative and liberal views. Moderate and swing voters were important for both candidates. Goldwater's acceptance speech became a classic example of how to alienate these voters. He said:

"Those who do not care for our cause, we don't expect to enter our ranks in any case. And let our Republicanism, so focused and so dedicated, not be made fuzzy and futile by unthinking and stupid labels. I would remind you that extremism in the defense of liberty is no vice. And let me remind you also that moderation in the pursuit of justice is no virtue." [6]

Courtesy Neville Colvin, 1964 Barry Goldwater and Lyndon Johnson Cartoon

The Senator from Arizona took six states and 52 electoral votes. The President won with 61 % of the popular vote and 486 electoral votes.

---

[6] Barry Goldwater, Republican Convention of 1964,
https://www.youtube.com/watch?v=RVNoClu0h9M

Senator Gary Hart, 1987, Courtesy Cornell University

In 1987, rumors began that Democratic front-runner, Gary Hart was having affairs. He challenged the media to, "Follow me around." They did. On May 3rd the Miami Herald reported a story about a woman who stayed with Hart.[7] He suspended his campaign a week after and ended his quest for the Presidency. A few weeks later the National Enquirer published a photo with him with his alleged girlfriend, Donna Rice, on vacation in Bimini.

---

[7] James Savage, THE GARY HART STORY: HOW IT HAPPENED, The Miami Herald on May 10, 1987 http://www.unc.edu/~pmeyer/Hart/hartarticle.html

Governor George Romney, Courtesy US Department of Housing and Urban Development

Michigan Governor George Romney was an early favorite for the Republican nomination for President in 1968. He was the only anti-Vietnam war Republican candidate among the field that included Ronald Reagan, Nelson Rockefeller and Richard Nixon. During a TV interview, Romney claimed that his early support of the war was a result of "brainwashing." He said, "When I came back from Vietnam I just had the greatest brainwashing that anyone can get. Not only by the generals, but also by the diplomatic corps over there. They do a very thorough job." Following the comment, his campaign began to slide.[8]

---

[8] Eric Black | 12/02/11Politics by gaffe: recalling the 'brainwashing' of George Romney, Minneapolis Post, http://www.minnpost.com/eric-black-ink/2011/12/politics-gaffe-recalling-brainwashing-george-romney

Vice President Al Gore, Courtesy Library of Congress

"During my service in the United States Congress, I took the initiative in creating the Internet." This statement by Tennessee Democrat Al Gore in a CNN interview on March 9th, 1999, cast an image as an exaggerator which damaged his prospects for the election.[9]

---

[9] Glenn Kessler November 4, 2013A cautionary tale for politicians: Al Gore and the 'invention' of the Internet, The Washington Posthttps://www.washingtonpost.com/blogs/fact-checker/wp/2013/11/04/a-cautionary-tale-for-politicians-al-gore-and-the-invention-of-the-internet/

Arkansas Governor Bill Clinton and President George Bush during the 1992 Campaign, Courtesy Library of Congress

George H.W. Bush won the Republican nomination for President in 1988. During his acceptance speech, he said, "Read my lips: no new taxes." The phrase became an important part of his campaign which he won.

Item: Former President Bush endorses McCain...

Courtesy Dave Granlund, Metro West Daily News

As President, the line hurt him when a rise in taxes was proposed to lower the budget deficit. Bush agreed to the increase. He regretted the decision during the 1992 campaign for the Republican nomination when his opponent, Pat Buchanan, used it consistently as an example of broken promises. That year, President Bush was defeated in his bid for a second term by Arkansas Governor William Jefferson Clinton.

President Richard Nixon, Courtesy, Atlantic

To commemorate the 40th anniversary of Richard Nixon's "last press conference," Ethan Rarick of the San Francisco Chronicle wrote this on December 1st, 2002:[10]

On the morning after losing a bid to become governor of California in 1962, Richard Nixon bitterly bid farewell to the political world and the troublesome press corps that chronicled it: "You won't have Nixon to kick around anymore."

Usually that "last press conference" is read as a reflection of the man, a hint of the paranoid style that would mark Nixon's presidency.

Even if elected to office, what he or she has said and done in the past may foretell how they will govern. Their statements could also force the Administration to be on the defensive fighting misstatements and ghosts of the past when they need to concentrate resources on the future.

---

[10] Ethan Rarick, San Francisco Chronicle, Kicking Nixon Around Some More, December 1st 2002, http://www.sfgate.com/politics/article/Kicking-Nixon-around-some-more-Tricky-Dick-s-2749199.php

We need to look cautiously at those candidates who speak without self-control and play loose and fast with facts. It will come back to haunt them and those who voted for them.

Personal Presence

"A leader must be engaged with those they lead. This deals with constituents and customers and followers. Lincoln visited his cabinet heads, stayed with the troops, was on the battlefield. He went to Richmond, immediately after the treaty was signed to end the Civil War, to sit in the chair of Jefferson Davis. He did not cheer or gloat over victory. He was there as a symbol to those who fought, died and sacrificed. He represented compassion, understanding and a singular commitment to the ideals that were struggled over. Eminent leaders are personally present and out front and look and exhibit that they are in command. They meet with their teams, discuss issues and have the discipline to show engagement at all levels. Some may call it casting a perception of leadership. Others say it is cultivating charisma. Others consider it managing power.

To a large extent, it is the rigor to create a self-image that adheres to rules which lead to better handling of the decision-making process. Presidents, Prime Ministers, celebrities and captains of industry and business, look to portray a persona in the eyes of those they command and those who look to them as models. All eyes are on them. Leaders need to be cognizant of living in a 'fish bowl.' All see how they are. Their lives and personal conduct must reflect the sincerity of their words and actions.

By being personally engaged with their teams, great leaders help develop their subordinates into future leaders. They gain loyalty and respect. Great leaders are accessible and available. When associates stop doing this, then the leader no longer leads."[11]

The Blackmail Factor

We cannot afford to have in the Presidency someone with a questionable background who has played loose with morals. Some feel that the sexual escapades of a President are a private affair. They are not. Neither are their financial affairs or other activities that could affect the trust the public and the world has in them. The President, or any high level public official for that matter, can be "blackmailed." Imagine if political enemies or foreign powers knew of a President's extra marital affairs and used this information to alter vital public policy. It could affect the future of the nation and the world and put in jeopardy countless lives.

It is clear: words and behavior in and out of the Oval Office matter.

---

[11] Emilio Iodice, Profiles in Leadership from Caesar to Modern Times, North American Business Press, Miami, Florida, 2013, p. 282

Understanding the Big Issues Facing the President in 2016

The candidates will distinguish themselves by their grasp of the major issues that attract voters' attention. The key ones include the following:

Short Term

"It's the Economy, Stupid"

Courtesy Chan Lowe/Tribune Content Agency US News

Jobs, jobs, jobs. The memory of the Great Recession will linger in voters' minds. Without a robust economy nothing can be solved. A May, 2015 Gallup Poll reported the following:[12]

Eighty-six percent of Americans say the economy will be extremely or very important to their vote next year, a significantly higher percentage than for any other issue. Concerns about terrorism rank high at 74% with foreign affairs further down the list at 61%.

The poll found that the economy was the principle issue for both Democrat and Republican voters. Others came into play in the study as demonstrated from the following Gallup chart:[13]

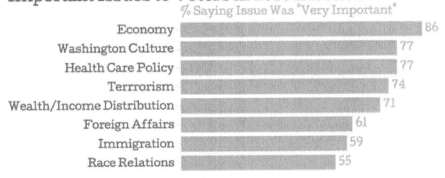

Important Issues to Voters in 2016 Election
% Saying Issue Was "Very Important"

Issue	%
Economy	86
Washington Culture	77
Health Care Policy	77
Terrrorism	74
Wealth/Income Distribution	71
Foreign Affairs	61
Immigration	59
Race Relations	55

US NEWS   Lindsey Cook for USN&WR; Source: Gallup

The findings indicate that financial security still ranks as the most important preoccupation facing voters even in good times. Issues like the importance of terrorism and short term foreign crises that could affect the American homeland are important but will not resonate with voters as much as the economy.

---

[12] Jeffrey Jones, Gallup, Important Issues to Voters in the 2016 Election, May 6-7, 2015.
http://www.gallup.com/poll/183164/economy-trumps-foreign-affairs-key-2016-election-issue.aspx

[13] Ibid. as reported in US News and World Report by Lindsey Cook June 29, 2015.

Courtesy Steve Breen—Creators Syndicate, US News

The middle class has been especially hard hit during this recession and it is this group that will have the largest impact on who the next President will be. Often times "populist" candidates, who appeal to middle class and lower class voters, offer simple ideas and concepts to resolve problems. No populist President has been elected since the middle of the 19th century.[14] In the majority of cases, centrist candidates who follow a middle of the road theme are elected.

Currently, the percentage of adults in jobs is lower than it was when Jimmy Carter was President in the late 1970s. It should not be surprising that this has created anger among voters which is fueling

---

[14] Edward Luce, Financial Times, October 5, 2015, It's still the Middle Class, Dumbo. http://www.ft.com/intl/cms/s/0/aa5eb462-68fe-11e5-a57f-21b88f7d973f.html?ftcamp=crm/email/2015105/nbe/Comment/product#axzz3ngJUdz00

populism in the 2016 campaign. Charismatic candidates offering quick solutions will resonate in times like these.

For 2016, the condition of labor will be the key to who enters the White House. Some project that wages will be stronger by Election Day. This will reduce the possibilities of a populist winning. Chances are that conditions will be the same in November, 2016 as they are at the end of 2015. Whoever wins in 2016, will face daunting economic and foreign policy challenges. We need to make sure he or she is fit for the job.

Medium and Long Term Challenges

Climate change, pandemics, environmental problems, public and consumer debt, gun control and concerns about China's economy and other medium and long term questions will be discussed during the campaign. It is essential to study the policies of the candidates and determine if they supply solutions and not concepts that could create more problems.

The Environment

Courtesy Steve Benson, The Arizona Republic USA Today

Whether or not one believes in global warming is not the issue. International environmental challenges are, however. They affect the air we breathe and the water we drink. We cannot rest our laurels with strong US laws of the past while China destroys the planet today. Global cooperation is vital. No Administration will be successful in dealing with critical ecological questions unless they know how to harness transnational support.

In 2014 Pew Research Center found that a majority of American adults favor stricter controls to address climate change. The opinions vary depending on party affiliation. A majority of Democrats want stronger requirements while Republicans prefer less. What is clear is that a large group of voters, including many independents, are looking for action on climate change.[15] They are also concerned about foreign affairs.

Most new Presidents are weak in foreign policy. If this is the case, they have to demonstrate the ability to learn quickly and bring in experts who will be capable to tackle the deadly issues of global terrorism before they reach our door step. This is where the Presidential Brain Trust comes in. Who will pick the best experts to help deal with our most pressing international challenges? This is the critical question. Facing the growing threat of the Islamic State of Iraq and Syria (ISIS) is an example of what the next President will confront.

ISIS's Plans for a Nuclear Weapon

Courtesy Michael Ramirez, *Investors Business Daily.*

---

[15] Steven Cohen, Executive Director, Columbia University's Earth Institute, The Environment and the 2016 Elections, August 10th, 2015, http://www.huffingtonpost.com/steven-cohen/the-environment-and-the-2_b_7965156.html

The day after the ISIS attacks on Paris that happened on November 13th, 2015, Journalists Karen Yourish, Derek Watkins and Tom Giratkanon wrote an article in the New York Times entitled: *Paris Bloodshed May Be the Latest of Many ISIS Attacks Around the World*. They quoted former CIA operations officer Patrick M. Skinner. He noted that the Paris attacks were "choreographed" and:

"The fact that they could do this, especially in Paris, where the intelligence service is really good, clearly there's a hole somewhere," Mr. Skinner said.

The Islamic State has been expanding beyond its base in Iraq and Syria since it declared a caliphate, or Islamic state, in June 2014. The group is focused on three parallel tracks, according to Harleen Gambhir, an analyst at the Institute for the Study of War:

- inciting regional conflict with attacks in Iraq and Syria;
- building relationships with jihadist groups that can carry out military operations across the Middle East and North Africa;
- and inspiring, and sometimes helping, ISIS sympathizers to conduct attacks in the West.

'The goal," Ms. Gambhir said, 'is that through these regional affiliates and through efforts to create chaos in the wider world, the organization will be able to expand, and perhaps incite a global apocalyptic war.'"[16]

Two decades ago reports of the results of the collapse of the former Soviet Union included what happened to the "evil empire's" vast

---

[16] KAREN YOURISH, DEREK WATKINS and TOM GIRATIKANON, Paris Bloodshed May Be the Latest of Many ISIS Attacks Around the World, New York Times, Nov. 14, 2015

nuclear arsenal. The superpower's cache of atomic weapons was scattered across several countries without the ability to control them. Professor Graham T. Allison of Harvard's Kennedy School was the author of *"Nuclear Terrorism: The Ultimate Preventable Catastrophe."* In 1996 he explained that the fall of Russia's command and control society left nothing secure: "The Russian nuclear weapons archipelago includes hundreds of sites over one-seventh of the Earth's land mass, sites at which 1,000 tons of highly enriched uranium, 100 tons of plutonium and some 30,000 nuclear warheads are at risk."[17] Journalist Douglas Birch in *Foreign Policy* said even more: "Russia inherited [the Soviet Union's] vast stores of nuclear, chemical, and biological weapons. And they were a mess. Western visitors to weapons depots and labs were shocked to find AWOL guards, broken fences and unlocked doors. Two million nerve gas shells were discovered sitting in rotting barns in a patch of forest in western Siberia."[18]

Since then, the US spent billions to help Russia improve its security at nuclear facilities and assist in decommissioning or destroying thousands of nuclear war heads. The cooperation with Russia to continue the effort ended in 2014. Today, radioactive materials to create a "dirty bomb" are still relatively easy to obtain and transport. The threat of radiation sickness for a suicide bomber is of little concern.

---

[17] Kathy Gilsinan, Why Moldova May Be the Scariest Country on Earth, A new report details a black market in nuclear materials. The Atlantic, Oct 8, 2015
http://www.theatlantic.com/international/archive/2015/10/moldova-nuclear-weapons-isis/409456/

[18] Ibid Kathy Gilsinan,

Courtesy Nate Beeler, *The Columbus Dispatch.*

In October, 2015, the Associated Press published a startling report about the criminal networks in the former Soviet Union attempting to sell radioactive materials to Middle Eastern extremists. The center of the activity was Moldova. The information came from sting operations conducted by the FBI and local authorities. It was discovered that the criminals involved had enough radioactive material to create weapons of mass destruction. Reports from other sources give credence to the rising concern of ISIS, in particular, hoarding highly processed uranium to make a bomb.

Australian Foreign Minister, Julie Bishop, has stated that NATO is preoccupied about lethal materials in the hands of ISIS that could produce chemical weapons or something worse.[19] The most recent information came from Moldova where investigations continue.

---

[19] Adam Withnall, ISIS's Dirty Bomb: Jihadists have seized 'enough radioactive material to build their first WMD',Nato and the Australia Group 'really worried' by latest defense reports, The Independent, Wednesday, June 10th, 2015

"Moldova has taken many important steps to strengthen its counter nuclear smuggling capabilities," said Eric Lund, spokesman for the State Department's bureau in charge of nonproliferation. 'The arrests made by Moldovan authorities in 2011 for the attempted smuggling of nuclear materials are a good example of how Moldova is doing its part.'

Wiretapped conversations exposed plots that targeted the United States, the Moldovan officials said. In one case, a middleman said it was essential the smuggled bomb-grade uranium go to Arabs, said Malic, an investigator in all four sting operations. He said: 'I really want an Islamic buyer because they will bomb the Americans.'"[20]

---

[20] Associated Press, The Smugglers Help ISIS Make a Dirty Bomb, October, 7th, 2015, http://nypost.com/2015/10/07/the-smugglers-trying-to-help-isis-make-a-dirty-bomb/

Education

Courtesy Marshall Ramsey, The (Jackson, Miss.) Clarion-Ledger

In 4 years an active and popular leader can launch programs that take hold in the medium to long run. Education is one of them. We need a "Landing a Man on the Moon" approach. America should be the first in education in the world beginning at Kindergarten. Tomorrow's leaders are in first grade today. Look carefully at those candidates who propose improvements in education.

The Urgent Need to Reform Campaign Financing

A June, 2015 survey by the New York Times and CBS News showed that "money holds far too much sway and that sweeping changes are needed in our political system. A full 85 percent of respondents said our current system is so flawed that it needs to either see fundamental changes or be rebuilt completely…Voters don't want small tweaks to an otherwise functioning system. The message coming through is a far-reaching call for reform: the system is *broken*… Support for restricting campaign donations among Republicans polled was almost as strong as support among Democrats polled."[21] At the same time, 60% of those polled were skeptical that anything would be done. These finding cut across all age groups including younger voters. Millennials, i.e. those in the 18-29 age group, reflect the same sort of cynicism when it comes to beliefs about the way the political system work. For the last 15 years, the Harvard Institute of Politics (IOP) has studied millennial thinking. Recent results show they are growing more skeptical about candidates, political parties and campaign financing than in the past. At the same time, they vote less than other age groups unless political parties and candidates reach out to them specifically as President Obama did during the 2008 campaign. They may be a pivotal factor in a close election.

The high cost of campaigns forces candidates to seek funds from private groups. Where this clashes with the need to honestly and

---

[21] Marge Baker, Overwhelming Majority of Americans Want Campaign Finance Overhaul, Moyers and Company, June 5, 2015, http://billmoyers.com/2015/06/05/overwhelming-majority-americans-want-campaign-finance-overhaul/

equitably conduct the public business and fulfill the public trust democracy is denied.

Courtesy John Cole, The Times-Tribune

"But while ordinary citizens overwhelmingly want tax breaks for the middle class, better wages and mandatory sick leave, many politicians are not interested in passing these reforms - because the super-wealthy individuals and powerful special interests funding our elections do not."[22] Recent Supreme Court rulings are blamed for the current situation. Paul Gordon of Moyers and Company commented on the rulings this way: "They acknowledge that laws

---

[22] Katie Rose Quandt, Why Campaign Finance Reform Is the First Issue That We Must Address, Moyers & Company, January, 25th, 2015

can be passed to prevent corruption and its appearance, but they have reduced that concept to little more than outright bribery."[23]

Courtesy Mike Luckovich, Atlanta Journal-Constitution

The perception is that politicians are beholden to their donors and not to their constituents who put them in office and pay their salaries. "And as long as special interest groups and extremely wealthy individuals continue to bankroll campaigns, they'll be the only ones getting what they want."[24]

~

Thomas Friedman summed up what the next President will face in an Op-ed column in the New York Times of November 11th, 2015, entitled, *Voters, You Can Have Everything*:

---

[23] Ibid. Marge Baker, Moyers and Company
[24] Ibid Quandt, Moyers and Compary

Alas, though, the next president will not be governing in fantasy — but with some cruel math. So the gap between this campaign and the morning after is likely to make for one really cold shower.

Start with geopolitics. The size of the governance hole that would have to be filled to simultaneously destroy the Islamic State, or ISIS, defeat Syria's dictator, Bashar al-Assad, and rebuild Syria, Iraq, Yemen and Libya into self-sustaining governments is staggering. And yet the cost of doing too little — endlessly bleeding refugees into our allies Turkey, Jordan, Lebanon and the European Union — is also astronomical. When the cost of action and the cost of inaction both feel unaffordable, you have a wicked problem.

Not only do the tax-cutting plans offered by the leading Republican candidates create eye-popping deficits, but some Democratic tax hike proposals don't quite add up, either. As the Washington Post economics columnist Robert Samuelson reported last week, a Brookings Institution study found that even if the top income tax rate were increased to 50 percent from 39.6 percent, it would cover less than a quarter of the deficit for the 2015 fiscal year, let alone generate funds for increased investment.

If we want to invest now in more infrastructure — as we should do — and make sure we don't overburden the next generation to pay for all the retiring baby boomers, something will have to give, or as Samuelson put it: "If middle-class Americans need or want bigger government, they will have to pay for it. Sooner or later, a tax increase is coming their way. There is no tooth fairy."

And finally, with carbon dioxide levels in the atmosphere having just reached heights not seen in millennium, if we want to "manage the unavoidable" effects of climate change and "avoid the unmanageable" ones, it will surely require a price on carbon — soon.

So enjoy the fun of this campaign while it lasts, because the next president will not be governing in poetry or prose or fantasy — but with excruciating trade-offs. The joke is on us.

Chapter Three: A Great Country Needs Great Leaders

There is nothing wrong with America that cannot be cured by what is right with America. **William J. Clinton**

What the people want is very simple. They want an America as good as its promise. **Barbara Jordan**

This nation will remain the land of the free only so long as it is the home of the brave. **Elmer Davis**

This country will not be a good place for any of us to live in unless we make it a good place for all of us to live in. **T. Roosevelt**

America is a nation with many flaws, but hopes so vast that only the cowardly would refuse to acknowledge them. **James Michener**

When an American says that he loves his country, he means not only that he loves the New England hills, the prairies glistening in the sun, the wide and rising plains, the great mountains, and the sea. He means that he loves an inner air, an inner light in which freedom lives and in which a man can draw the breath of self-respect... America is much more than a geographical fact. It is a political and moral fact — the first community in which men set out in principle to institutionalize freedom, responsible government, and human equality. **Adlai Stevenson**

If our country is worth dying for in time of war let us resolve that it is truly worth living for in time of peace. **Hamilton Fish**

America was born in outrageous ambition, so bold as to be improbable. The deprived, the oppressed, and the powerless from all over the globe came here with little more than the desire to realize themselves. **Mario Cuomo**

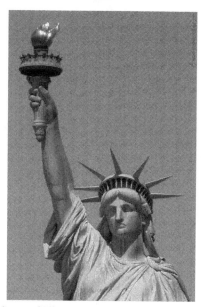

Statue of Liberty Courtesy National Archives

Often times, candidates claim that they should be selected to the highest office in the land to "make America great again." This assumes that the United States is no longer a country of opportunity and freedom, providing an environment for individual and collective aspirations to be realized. This is not the case if we examine who we are today, where we have been and where we are going in the context of our American identity.

A July 3rd, 2014 article in the Times of San Diego by Len Novarro,[25] entitled: *America: What Makes it Great,* outlined these factors:

Technology and Creativity: Some of the greatest inventions of all time have been created by Americans. From Thomas Edison to Steve Jobs, from light bulbs to the internet we have constantly developed new ideas for the world. Look at Silicon Valley's

---

[25] Len Novarro, What Makes America Great, Times of San Diego, July 3rd, 2014. (http://timesofsandiego.com/opinion/2014/07/03/america-makes-great/)

billionaires to see how much more is to come from America. Look at how many Americans continue to win the Noble Prize.

Diversity, Tolerance, Individualism: The Statue of Liberty says: "Give me your tired, your poor, your huddled masses yearning to breathe free..." We have embraced immigrants, and people of all faiths and nationalities who want a better life, including our Native Americans, who inspired us with their desire to work and generosity. We tolerate each other despite out differences. We are not perfect but seek perfection. We live together in peace which is not the case in many parts of the world. Ours is not a class system. Wealth has its influence but we still have a society where we can determine our own course.

Economy and Entrepreneurship: We still manage the largest economy on earth that promotes small business and self-made people. If wealth is a measure, America has more millionaires and billionaires than any other country. We still have the highest standard of living in the world.

Our System of Law: Democracy and respect for the law and fairness are part of the American system of government. Our institutions exist to protect the grand and the humble.

Education: It is not perfect and needs constant improvement, yet our system of education attracts people from the entire globe.

Music and Entertainment: The American contribution to music and movies is enormous and continues to grow.

A Nation of Beauty: From coast to coast and from the Great Lakes to the Gulf of Mexico, the US is a country of contrasts and great beauty.

Cities: Some of the most interesting cities on earth are in America. New York, San Francisco, Los Angeles, Chicago, Miami, New Orleans, Boston, and Seattle, for example, are all different and full of life and culture.

Sense of Morality and Social Consciousness: We bring out our problems so we can do something about them. We have a sense of doing the right thing despite the obstacles we face to do so.

Remember the Greatest Generation: What made them great? They faced huge problems first of poverty in the Depression than winning the War. They defeated poverty and Nazism. The leaders of that era were not afraid to ask us to sacrifice for a cause they were willing to die for. It was that generation that pulled the country together and it was those leaders who said, "Follow Me."

Resilience: After almost 250 years of trials, tribulations and progress we are still here in much the same form created by the American Revolution.

In the movie, *Independence Day*, the President said, "We can't be consumed by our petty differences anymore. We will be united in our common interests…We will not go quietly into the night."

Finally, Gary Shapiro, CEO of the Consumer Electronics Association wrote this in a July 12, 2012 article in Forbes, [26] entitled: *Is America the Greatest Country in the World?*

"I am passionate that our nation was, still is and can remain the best in world. We not only owe it to our children to act to preserve our greatness, but we must also honor those who have served and risked their life and limb in our Armed Forces to preserve our nation and its freedoms.

We are a beacon for the world. Our challenge is not to lament our decline or even celebrate our exceptionalism; it is to come together with true leadership that can unite us as we sacrifice to preserve and expand our greatness."

---

[26] Gary Shapiro, Is America the Greatest Country in the World?, Forbes, July 12th, 2012.
//www.forbes.com/sites/garyshapiro/2012/07/25/is-america-the-greatest-country-in-the-world/

Courtesy Pat Oliphant, Cartoon of September 13th, 2001, Universal Uclick

Part Two: Leadership Qualities the President MUST HAVE.

Chapter One: Reformer

There is a need for financial reform along ethical lines that would produce in its turn an economic reform to benefit everyone. This would nevertheless require a courageous change of attitude on the part of political leaders. **Pope Francis**

To live for a principle, for the triumph of some reform by which all mankind are to be lifted up to be wedded to an idea may be, after all, the holiest and happiest of marriages. **Elizabeth Cady Stanton**

Whenever anything extraordinary is done in American municipal politics, whether for good or for evil, you can trace it almost invariably to one man. The people do not do it. Neither do the 'gangs,' 'combines,' or political parties. **Lincoln Steffens**

Let my name stand among those who are willing to bear ridicule and reproach for the truth's sake, and so earn some right to rejoice when the victory is won. **Louisa May Alcott**

Men must be capable of imagining and executing and insisting on social change if they are to reform or even maintain civilization, and capable too of furnishing the rebellion which is sometimes necessary if society is not to perish of immobility. **Rebecca West**

[Bram Stoker] wrote in his diary: "(Theodore Roosevelt) Must be President someday. A man you can't cajole, can't frighten, can't buy." **Edmund Morris, *The Rise of Theodore Roosevelt***

"Nobody cares how much you know until they know how much you care." **Theodore Roosevelt**

President Theodore Roosevelt, Courtesy Library of Congress

One of the words most frequently used in Presidential politics is "reform." Candidates invariably claim that they will be the ones to reform the system. In nearly each election cycle in the last 30 years they have focused on health care reform, tax reform, immigration reform, campaign financing reform, entitlement reform, etc. Some progress has been made in these areas but arguably, more needs to be done. What is obvious is that one trait that is essential to be an effective American President, particularly in 2016, is to be a true and experienced reformer. Take the perennial issue of campaign finance reform as an example.

Theodore Roosevelt fought to reform the method of financing and conducting political campaigns as far back as 1881 as a New York State Assemblyman.

Theodore Roosevelt: Civil Service, Campaign and Economic Reform

In the 2015 Mission Statement of the US Office of Personnel Management, there is the biography of Theodore Roosevelt. He is considered the greatest Civil Service Commissioners in American history.   As Commissioner, Roosevelt accomplished major revisions to the way the Federal Government functioned and hired public servants and especially the operation of the "spoils system,"[27]

With unbridled courage, zeal, and tenacity, Theodore Roosevelt worked to ensure a hiring system for America's government workers based on fairness and equal access and protection for all—making him the undisputed father of today's Federal Service... During his term as United States Civil Service Commissioner (1889-1895) the full force of his energy, enthusiasm, and aggressiveness was put to the task of building up the Federal civil service system.

He undertook the task of reform with the same honesty and zeal that he showed for all of his endeavors. Commissioner Roosevelt believed his role was to create a civil service system that would attract the best people into government.

Roosevelt's principles to reform the system were based on three standards: nondiscrimination and opportunities for all citizens; merit based appointments and shielding public servants from punishment because of their political beliefs. He led the fight to expose corrupt officials and toiled against waste, fraud and abuse. On one occasion, he personally recommended the removal of New York board examiners who sold test questions to the public for $50. He had Baltimore postal officials arrested for buying votes for the re-election of the man who had appointed him to his position, President Benjamin Harrison. His courage and tenacity assured that civil service laws would be permanently enforced no matter what political affiliation.[28]

---

[27] US Office of Personnel Management, Mission Statement 2015, https://www.opm.gov/about-us/our-mission-role-history/theodore-roosevelt/
[28] Ibid. Office of Personnel Management

Courtesy National Archives

As President, Theodore Roosevelt led one of the greatest expansions and modernizations of the government. The competitive civil service grew from 110,000 to 235,000. As a result, the merit system far surpassed the spoils system in numbers in the federal hiring.

NO MOLLY-CODDLING HERE

Courtesy National Archives

He fought to control monopolistic power in business; created the Departments of Commerce and Labor, added 150 million acres of public lands to be conserved as part of the nation's national parks and proposed and signed new laws to regulate the pharmaceutical industry and rules to protect the health of the people of America. Roosevelt's 1906 Pure Food and Drug Act remains the foundation of the US system of health into the 21st century.

The Office of President Theodore Roosevelt, 1904, Courtesy Library of Congress

Roosevelt built the West Wing of the White House to be the executive office of the President which today houses the Oval Office. His changes ushered in the modern American Presidency.

An issue that is being discussed actively in the 2016 election is altering the way we finance campaigns. Beth Rowen, in an article in the 2015 online version of the Infoplease Almanac, entitled *Campaign-Finance Reform: History and Timeline* [29] wrote the following:

Over the past several decades, political campaigns in the U.S. have become increasingly costly and unsavory. Nevertheless, campaign finance remains a divisive issue. Proponents of campaign finance limits argue that wealthy donors and corporations hold too much sway in elections and as a result, corrupt campaigns. Those favoring less regulation contend that campaign donations are a form of free speech.

---

[29] Beth Rowen, Infoplease Almanac 2015, Campaign Finance Reform: History and Timeline. http://www.infoplease.com/us/history/campaign-finance-reform-timeline.html)

Campaign finance legislation dates to 1867, but the regulation of campaign fundraising didn't become a major issue until the early 20th century, prompted by the presidential election of 1896, which introduced a new era of campaign advertising and the custom of seeking donations from businesses.

The Whiff of Corruption in Campaigns Not a New Phenomenon

Patronage was prevalent in early campaigns, and the spoils system was in full swing by the time Andrew Jackson took office in 1828. Jackson was famous for appointing contributors to plum positions in his administration. The spoils system factored into the assassination of James Garfield. One of the president's supporters and speech writers, Charles Guiteau, shot and killed Garfield after being denied a post in his administration. The assassination led to passage of the Pendleton Act of 1883, which required that civil service positions be filled based on merit and exam results rather than party affiliation.

Vote-buying was another form of corruption in early presidential races. Political parties and candidates printed their own ballots and often paid voters to submit them. The government didn't take responsibility for printing ballots until 1896.

The movement to rein in campaign fundraising and spending gathered steam once again after Watergate, when corruption in politics reached its peak and public confidence in public officials hit a nadir.

There have been Presidents who have been successful in changing the system to right wrongs and correct abuses to the political process. This is one quality that is needed especially with challenges that seem impossible to overcome like campaign financing, immigration reform and tax reform. It has been attempted in the past, not always successfully.

Beth Rowen, in the article previously cited, outlined some of the legislation of the past that worked to reform the system of financing political campaigns. During the administration of Theodore Roosevelt (1900-1908), for example, the Tillman Act was passed to prohibit corporations and national banks from financing Presidential and congressional campaigns. It was the first law to regulate federal campaigns but was filled with loopholes that made it less effective than originally planned. The first federal campaign disclosure law was passed in 1910 during the term of William Howard Taft (1908-1912). The Federal Corrupt Practices Act required candidates for the House of Representatives to disclose the source of all contributions and report on campaign spending. It was later amended to require Senators to adhere to the same guidelines.

Restrictions were tightened with legislation leading almost to the present day. In recent years, major reversals from Supreme Court decisions have once again resulted in demands for reform.

Byron Tau, in an April 22nd, 2015 article in the Wall Street Journal entitled, *Campaign Finance Reform, An Enduring Election Promise,* explained the following: [30]

After the 2002 Bipartisan Campaign Reform Act, some campaign cash started flowing to outside groups that were required under law to remain independent of parties and candidates. In exchange for that independence, they could spend freely. In 2004 and 2008, these groups were called "527s."

In subsequent years federal courts have affirmed and expanded the right of outside groups to spend in politics, and super PAC and the 501(c) 4 nonprofit became their favored vehicles.

Since then, critics of the system have proposed a constitutional amendment to give Congress the power to regulate and stem the flow of money into politics.

"The flood of dark money into our nation's political system poses the greatest threat to our democracy that I have witnessed during my time in public service," Sen. Harry Reid (D., Nevada) said at a hearing last year.

Reid's statement is telling. The lifeblood of democracy is citizen participation with government held accountable to the people. Our current system of campaign financing depends on big contributors. It has weakened public participation and accountability. Low voter turnouts even in high profiles elections, cynicism and lack of trust in politicians and the political process is rampant in the face of the influence of from wealthy contributors and scandals involving campaign contributions. The next President must change the system if democracy is to survive and advance in America.

---

[30] Byron Tau, *Campaign Finance Reform, An Enduring Election Promise,* April 22nd, 2015 Wall Street Journal (http://blogs.wsj.com/washwire/2015/04/22/campaign-finance-reform-an-enduring-election-promise/)

Abraham Lincoln, 1860, Courtesy Library of Congress

Abraham Lincoln and the Emancipation Proclamation

A house divided against itself cannot stand." I believe this government cannot endure permanently half slave and half free. I do not expect the Union to be dissolved – I do not expect the house to fall – but I do expect it will cease to be divided. It will become all one thing, or all the other.

63

As I would not be a slave, so I would not be a master. This expresses my idea of democracy. Whatever differs from this, to the extent of the difference, is no democracy.

It is the eternal struggle between two principles – right and wrong – throughout the world. They are the two principles that have stood face to face from the beginning of time; and will ever continue to struggle. The one is the common right of humanity, and the other the divine right of kinds. It is the same principle in whatever shape it develops itself.

Let us have faith that right makes might, and in that faith let us the end dare to do our duty as we understand it.

In giving freedom to the slave, we assure freedom to the free - honorable alike in what we give, and what we preserve. We shall nobly save, or meanly lose, the last best hope of earth. Other means may succeed; this could not fail. The way is plain, peaceful, generous, just - a way which, if followed, the world will forever applaud, and God must forever bless.

I have always thought that all men should be free; but if any should be slaves it should be first those who desire it for themselves, and secondly those who desire it for others. **Lincoln**

Courtesy Harper's Weekly, November 17th, 1860

Dr. Ronald C. White is the foremost biographer of Abraham Lincoln today. His marvelous work, A. Lincoln: A Biography (Random House, New York, 2009) was reviewed by Ariel Gonzalez of the Miami Herald. He described our sixteenth President this way:

"Abraham Lincoln was less qualified to assume the presidency than any of his 15 predecessors. A self-educated lawyer with only two years in Congress under his belt, he had no executive, diplomatic or military experience (aside from a few uneventful months in the Illinois state militia). Even so, he successfully led the nation through its worst crisis… Lincoln's moral and intellectual development equipped him with the tools he needed for greatness."

It was those skills that gave him the wisdom and courage to fight to preserve the individual and collective liberty contained in the American Constitution and Declaration of Independence.

When Abraham Lincoln joined the newly formed Republican Party, he embraced its principles of reform. They stressed the personal growth of the individual to enjoy freedom and economic opportunity no matter what class or station in life. It was believed that anyone could rise to attain the American dream and that government should work to promote it.

"We stand at once the wonder and admiration of the whole world," he said in 1856. He saw the Republican mission as, "This cause is that every man can make himself." Abraham Lincoln viewed liberty as the economic and social freedom to unleash the genius of the republic to allow all to remake themselves as they desired. He was the embodiment of this reform movement: "There is no permanent class of hired laborers amongst us," Lincoln insisted in 1859:

"Twenty-five years ago, I was a hired laborer. The hired laborer of yesterday, labors on his own account to-day; and will hire others to labor for him to-morrow. Advancement — improvement in condition — is the order of things in a society of equals." [31]

This opportunity had to be extended to all people who inhabited the American continent, including slaves.

[31] Lincoln, "Speech at Kalamazoo, Michigan" (August 27, 1856) and "Fragment on Free Labor" (September 17, 1859), in Collected Works, 2:364 and 3:462. https://www.gilderlehrman.org/history-by-era/lincoln/essays/lincoln

Writing the Emancipation Proclamation
Engraving, Baltimore, October 1862, Adalbert John Volk, artist *Courtesy of The Gilder Lehrman Collection, New York.*

The greatest act of political, social and economic reform of the 19ᵗʰ century was the abolition of slavery in America. The Emancipation Proclamation bore the name of Abraham Lincoln. Lincoln was not an abolitionist, yet he believed in eliminating slavery. It was Lincoln who worked vigorously, intensely and ruthlessly with a reluctant Congress to pass the 13ᵗʰ amendment to the Constitution which ended slavery. It was the major issue dividing the nation and led to the Civil War. His courage and tenacity as a reformer resulted in the end of human bondage in America.

In 2016, we need a courageous reformer who will tackle the great issues of our time that need to change. The range is vast. It goes from campaign financing to immigration to tax policy to a host of social issues that continue to be in the forefront of public and political concern. We require a President who can unite us to resolve to change what we have for decades said must be changed to make America stronger, fairer and freer.

"Always bear in mind that your own resolution to succeed is more important than any other one thing." **Abraham Lincoln**

Chapter Two: Experience

Experience is the teacher of all things. **Julius Caesar**

People grow through experience if they meet life honestly and courageously. This is how character is built. **Eleanor Roosevelt**

One thorn of experience is worth a whole wilderness of warning. **James Russell Lowell**

The only source of knowledge is experience. **Albert Einstein**

Washington, Jefferson and Lincoln, Courtesy Miller Center, University of Virginia,

The Presidency is not a Position for Trainees

The White House is not a place for "trainees." Decisions need to be made, at times, at the blink of an eye. The President must have the ability to quickly judge and decide. While there is no comparable job to that of President, there are roles that demand executive political skills that help provide preparation. This reduces the learning curve.

Theodore Roosevelt and Franklin Roosevelt, Governors of New York, Courtesy Miller Center, University of Virginia

The Governors

Seventeen of our Presidents have been state governors. Some have been exceptional and, arguably, among our most effective leaders. They include Thomas Jefferson (Virginia), James Monroe (Virginia), Grover Cleveland (New York), William McKinley (Ohio), Theodore Roosevelt (New York), Woodrow Wilson (New Jersey), Franklin Roosevelt (New York), Ronald Reagan (California), Bill Clinton (Arkansas) and George W. Bush (Texas). Of course, experience as governor of a large state is different from that of a smaller state. The more complex the state, the more comparable it will be to the setting in the White House. Bringing this form of executive political experience plus other important leadership qualities improves the chances of a successful presidency but does not assure them.

Neither Washington nor Lincoln was a state governor. They are exceptions. Washington brought respect, dignity, military and administrative experience and admiration as a founding father of our republic.   He was present from the Revolution to the Constitution. He understood the substance of the United States and articulated a vision for our future. Abraham Lincoln brought the wisdom of the prairie and the American heartland. He had little or no formal education but loved learning and was skilled in the art of understanding the human condition. What he lacked in experience and education he more than made up for with his qualities of compassion, vision, his willingness to make tough decisions and his spirit of self-sacrifice and dedication to the ideals of American democracy. Abraham Lincoln brought integrity, wisdom, and leadership to the White House as no one before or after him.

In February, 2015, the Brookings Institution in Washington, DC surveyed the members of the American Political Science Association on the topic of Presidential Greatness. The top ten were: Lincoln, Washington, Franklin Roosevelt, Theodore Roosevelt, Jefferson, Truman, Eisenhower, Clinton, Jackson, and Wilson.   The ten Presidents considered the worst were: Taylor, Nixon, George W. Bush, Tyler, Fillmore, Hoover, William Henry Harrison, Pierce, Andrew Johnson, Warren Harding and James Buchanan.[32]

---

[32] **Brookings Institution, February 13th, 2015, 2016 Election: Research Behind the Race ›** **Measuring Obama against the great presidents,** http://www.brookings.edu/blogs/fixgov/posts/2015/02/13-obama-measuring-presidential-greatness-vaughn-rottinghaus

Overall average rating for each American president (out of 100)

Rank	Order	President	Rating
1	16	Abraham Lincoln	95.27
2	1	George Washington	92.28
3	31	Franklin Delano Roosevelt	89.72
4	25	Theodore Roosevelt	82.44
5	3	Thomas Jefferson	80.05
6	32	Harry S. Truman	76.57
7	33	Dwight Eisenhower	75.43
8	41	Bill Clinton	69.66
9	7	Andrew Jackson	69.22
10	27	Woodrow Wilson	68.69
11	39	Ronald Reagan	67.47
12	35	Lyndon Baines Johnson	67.29
13	4	James Madison	65.68
14	34	John F. Kennedy	64.04
15	2	John Adams	63.25
16	5	James Monroe	62.86
17	40	George H.W. Bush	60.76
18	43	Barack Obama	58.24
19	11	James K. Polk	56.96
20	26	William Howard Taft	54.58
21	24	William McKinley	53.91
22	6	John Quincy Adams	53.44
23	22	Grover Cleveland	51.2
24	37	Gerald Ford	50.05
25	8	Martin Van Buren	47.13
26	38	Jimmy Carter	44.2
27	29	Calvin Coolidge	41.79
28	18	Ulysses S. Grant	41.32
29	23	Benjamin Harrison	40.91
30	19	Rutherford B. Hayes	40
31	20	James Garfield	39.45
32	21	Chester Arthur	39.28
33	12	Zachary Taylor	39.19
34	36	Richard Nixon	37.26
35	42	Geoge W. Bush	36.91
36	10	John Tyler	36.74
37	13	Millard Fillmore	32.44
38	30	Herbert Hoover	32
39	9	William Henry Harrison	28.66
40	14	Franklin Pierce	26.41
41	17	Andrew Johnson	25.72
42	28	Warren Harding	24.11
43	15	James Buchanan	18.43

BROOKINGS

What is clear is that experience per se is not enough to assure a successful President. The type, the length, breath, depth and relevancy of the experience is key as well as other qualities like bravery, good judgement and the ability to communicate and articulate a vision. An example is James Buchanan. He was, perhaps, one of the most experienced men to occupy the White House.

James Buchanan, President of the United States, 1856-1860, Courtesy Library of Congress

James Buchanan: One of our Most Experienced Presidents Considered one of our Worst Leaders

Buchanan was elected five times to the House of Representatives. He spent ten years in the Senate. He was Minister to Russia under President Andrew Jackson, Minister to Great Britain, during the administration of Franklin Pierce and the Secretary of State of President James K. Polk. His time abroad and in the capitol helped him secure the Democratic nomination for President in 1856. He was certainly a candidate who was knowledgeable and understood the role of President. He aspired to be compared to George Washington. Instead, Buchanan ranks among our worst Chief Executives in the eyes of many historians. [33]

The reason may lie in the fact that he spent most of his time outside the US when the great debates about sectional politics and slavery happened. He used diplomacy to maintain peace between the North

---

[33] Philip S. Klein, President James Buchanan: A Biography, American Political Biography Press, Newtown Connecticut, 1995, page. 305

and South which resulted in alienating both sides. He viewed secession as illegal but felt that going to war was also illegal. As a result, he failed to create a unifying principle that the Northern and Southern states could accept to preserve the Union.[34]

President Polk considered Buchanan a man who lacked judgement. His political enemies said most of his ventures failed to materialize like expansion of the Navy and Army. They claimed that he missed the key opportunities of his age by vetoing the Morrill Act and the Homestead Act. The first accelerated agriculture and engineering research and education and the later opened up the west. Both were signed into law by Abraham Lincoln a few years later. [35]

The Value of Business Experience

A number of Presidents had business experience before entering the White House. It is often believed that this could be of benefit to the position in the Oval Office. What we find is that it does not always translate into the kind of experience that fits well in the White House. Much more depends on other factors than just business experience per se.

---

[34] Ibid. Klein p. xviii.
[35] Ibid Klein, p. 62

President Abraham Lincoln with youngest son, Tad, Courtesy the Library of Congress

President Abraham Lincoln

Lincoln ran a general store and invented a device to raise riverboats over sandbars, making him the only President to receive a patent. He also operated a successful law practice. He was characterized by determination and resilience even in the face of chronic failure.

Courtesy the Library of Congress

President Warren G. Harding

At 19, Harding bought a small newspaper business in Ohio, The Marion Star. He managed the operation with his wife. It became a financial success.

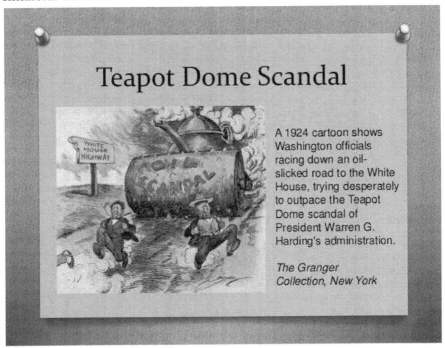

Courtesy the Granger Collection, New York and the National Archives

Harding, according to Presidential historians, ranks along with James Buchanan as among our least successful Presidents.

President Herbert Hoover with his dog, King Tut, Courtesy Library of Congress

President Herbert Hoover

After graduating from Stanford University with a degree in geology, Herbert Hoover started his own mining and engineering business in 1908. His company employed 175,000 people. It reorganized failing firms and invested in new projects.

Political Cartoon depicting Herbert Hoover's challenges, Courtesy National Archives

Hoover was elected to the White House in 1928. The Wall Street Crash happened a year later. He was unable to deal with the Great Depression that ensued. Millions lost their jobs and thousands of firms and institutions literally disappeared creating the worst economic and social crisis in US history. He was swept out of office by Franklin Roosevelt in the election of 1932.

Courtesy Library of Congress

President Franklin Delano Roosevelt

Franklin Roosevelt was still a young man when he was struck with infantile paralysis. He went to a resort in Warm Springs, Georgia to find relief. After a short time, he decided to invest part of his inherited trust fund into the operation to help others rise up from polio.

Poster featuring FDR to raise funds for Polio research, Courtesy Franklin Delano Roosevelt
Presidential Library

He created the Roosevelt Warm Springs Institute for Rehabilitation
in 1927. It is still operating today and is a center serving thousands
of patients each year.

March of Dimes Today, Courtesy Forbes Magazine

Courtesy the White House

President Harry Truman

When Harry Truman returned from France at the end of World War I he needed a job. He opened a clothing store with a wartime buddy. It flourished for a number of years but ended when a recession forced it to close.

Courtesy George W. Bush Presidential Library

President George W. Bush

President George W. Bush owned the Texas Rangers baseball team. He was very successful in increasing the value of his investment which made him a wealthy man.

Courtesy George H.W. Presidential Library

President George H.W. Bush

Following his time at Yale, the future 41st President, formed Bush-Overby Oil Development Company in 1951. In a few years, the firm merged with Zapata Petroleum resulting in a very successful venture.

Courtesy the Jimmy Carter Presidential Library

President Jimmy Carter

Jimmy Carter inherited a failing peanut farm when his father died in 1953. Carter resigned from the Navy to return to Georgia and take over the family business. He worked hard and diligently and applied strong management skills to produce a business that became prosperous.

Wendell Willkie: First Major Business Leader to Run for President

Wendell L. Willkie 1940, Courtesy Indiana Historical Society

I'm in business and proud of it...Nobody can make me soft-pedal any fact in my business career. After all, business is our way of life, our achievement, our glory.

The only soil in which liberty can grow is that of a united people. We must have faith that the welfare of one is the welfare of all. We must know that the truth can only be reached by the expression of our free opinions, without fear and without rancor. We must acknowledge that all are equal before God and before the law. And we must learn to abhor those disruptive pressures, whether religious, political, or economic, that the enemies of liberty employ.

When Winston Churchill became Prime Minister of England a few months ago, he made no sugar-coated promises. "I have nothing to offer you," he said, "but blood, tears, toil, and sweat." Those are harsh words, brave words; yet if England lives, it will be because her people were told the truth and accepted it. Fortunately, in America, we are not reduced to "blood and tears." But we shall not be able to avoid the "toil and sweat."

Wendell Willkie

He was the Republican Party nominee for President in 1940. Willkie was a business leader and proud of it. It was the first time in American history that someone of Willkie's background won the nomination for President from a major political party. He was a successful lawyer, World War I veteran and head of one of the largest electric utility companies in the country, Commonwealth and Southern. He was a former Democrat but changed his party affiliation during the New Deal. He actively opposed FDR's economic policies.

Without having any professional political experience, Willkie vigorously sought the nomination of the Republican Party for President in 1940. Not all Republicans were delighted to learn this. Willkie was a former Democrat and seeking the nomination of the opposing Party's highest office ran against the grain of the Republican Party's rank and file. A Senator from his home state of Indiana, James Watson, said he didn't mind if the town whore joined the church, but she should not lead the choir the first week.[36] The daughter of the late Republican President Theodore Roosevelt, Alice Roosevelt Longworth, said the Willkie campaign was "from the grass roots of ten thousand country clubs."[37] Willkie won the nomination on the sixth ballot at a highly charged Republican convention defeating several veteran politicians including Senators Robert A. Taft of Ohio and Arthur Vandenberg of Michigan and the young New York District Attorney, Thomas E.Dewey. The great issue during the convention was the war in Europe which began in 1939.

---

[36] Madison, James H. (February, 2001). "Willkie, Wendell Lewis". American National Biography. Retrieved November 5, 2015.
[37] Neal, Steve (1984). Dark Horse: A Biography of Wendell Willkie. Garden City, NY: Doubleday. P. 40

Wendell Willkie Campaign Poster, 1940, Courtesy Library of Congress

Willkie campaigned on the theme that he would be better able to handle a national emergency and would also bring the nation back to prosperity. He stressed that his business and executive leadership prepared him well to take on the economic and foreign policy challenges facing the nation. He styled himself after a common mid-westerner seeking the support of working class voters. FDR's Interior Secretary, Harold L. Ickes poked fun at Willkie by calling him "a simple, barefoot Wall Street lawyer."[38]

---

[38] Moe, Richard (2013). Roosevelt's Second Act. Oxford: Oxford University Press

Roosevelt had considered the idea of retiring but saw the war looming large in the destiny of the United States. He decided to seek an unprecedented third term. In the end, FDR was re-elected. Willkie received 45% of the popular vote but carried only nine states. When the outcome was clear, FDR confided to his son James: "I'm happy I've won, but I'm sorry Wendell lost."[39]

After the election, Willkie decided he would do all he could to support the President's efforts to aid Britain. He announced his support of the Lend-Lease Program on January 13th, 1941, only two months after conceding defeat to FDR. The President appreciated Willkie's talents and willingness to serve the country. FDR felt it was necessary to show bi-partisan support for the United Kingdom by sending the nominal head of the opposition Party as his emissary to support the British war effort. The Republicans were highly opposed to Lend-Lease. Willkie's announcement created a firestorm of protest against him from the Party regulars.

Nevertheless, he visited the President on the eve of FDR's third swearing in to discuss his new role. The President appointed him as his emissary to Britain and gave him a confidential letter to personally deliver to Winston Churchill. Willkie left for London three days later. His trip received great notoriety on both sides of the Atlantic. Willkie promised to do all he could to help Britain in her struggle against Nazi Germany. He saw the damage caused by the Blitzkrieg bombings of London, Coventry, Birmingham and Liverpool. He walked through the streets of London during Nazi raids and visited shelters. Churchill met with Willkie and recalled "a long talk with this most able and forceful man."[40] Willkie returned to the US. His mission was deemed a triumph.

---

[39] Ibid. P.179-180

[40] Ibid Neal, p.195-196

Willkie gave FDR full support for his efforts before and after Pearl Harbor. FDR decided to run for a fourth term. He wanted to remove Vice President Henry Wallace from the ticket. He sent an intermediary to ask Willkie if he would be interested in taking on the role. Willkie never responded. Instead, he made an attempt to secure the Republican nomination for President in 1944 but bowed out after a disappointing showing in the Wisconsin primary. Governor Thomas Dewey was the Republican nominee. Roosevelt once again won re-election.

Willkie and FDR talked about forming a new liberal party after the war. His vision and dreams were snuffed out when he suddenly died in October, 1944. Wendell Willkie was 52. His legacy was his staunch support of Roosevelt's plan to support Britain and his courage in the face of strong political opposition.

Susan Dunn wrote of Willkie: "He died as he had lived, an idealist, a humanitarian and a lone wolf." [41]   Steve Neal, Willkie's biographer explained something even more profound about him:

"Though he never became President, he had won something much more important, a lasting place in American history. Along with Henry Clay, William Jennings Bryan, and Hubert Humphrey, he was the also-ran who would be long remembered. 'He was a born leader,' wrote historian Allan Nevins, 'and he stepped up to leadership at just the moment when the world needed him.' Shortly before his death, Willkie told a friend, 'If I could write my own epitaph and if I had to choose between saying, 'Here lies an

---

[41] Dunn, Susan (2013). 1940: FDR, Willkie, Lindbergh, Hitler—the Election Amid the Storm. New Haven, CT: Yale University Press.p. 317

unimportant President,' or, 'Here lies one who contributed to saving freedom at a moment of great peril,' I would prefer the latter.'"[42]

The Concept of "Unfiltered Leaders"

Harvard University Professor, Gautam Mukunda, argues that experience in one role does not automatically transfer to a job like that of President of the United States. In an August 24th, 2012 article in Fortune Magazine, he wrote that Republican Party candidate Mitt Romney's business experience did not necessarily make him qualified to take on a political role:[43]

We have a lot of research that tells us experience doesn't transfer from one context to another very well. We know that when you bring stars from one company to another, even in the same industry, they usually don't stay stars. That's true even when you're moving within an industry. So think about how much more true it's going to be when you're moving from finance to politics…

The job of someone in a private equity fund is to maximize return on investors 'capital. He's incredibly good at that. But the job of president is not to maximize return on investors' capital. The president of the United States has 300 million people he has to benefit, and they have lots of different interests. Can he form coalitions with people who have no reason to work with him? Can he rally the public? Can he negotiate keeping in mind that he serves many, many different constituencies?

Are you saying that Romney's business experience would be a handicap, not an advantage?

It's both. The business experience tells us he's incredibly smart, he's hardworking, he's analytical. He's able to solve problems creatively and intelligently. These are all good things in a president. They should give us some confidence that we're not picking someone at random who has never done anything that would make you feel they're capable of being president. But at the same time it's a profoundly different set of skills.

Professor Makunda claims that those with business experience alone are prone to mistakes that politicians would not make. He believes that "unfiltered leaders"—those who haven't much relevant experience—will likely have a greater impact than filtered leaders. "What's harder to predict is whether that impact will be good or bad."[44] It can go either way.

---

[42] Neal, p. 324

[43] Fortune Magazine, August 24th, 2012, Do Presidents Need Experience by Gautam Mukunda. http://fortune.com/2012/08/24/do-presidents-need-experience/

[44] Ibid Mukunda

The First Lincoln-Douglas Debate, August 21st, 1858, Courtesy The Robinson Library and the
National Archives and Lincoln Home National Historic Site

Abraham Lincoln spent less time in politics than his competitor for
the Presidency in 1860, Stephan A. Douglas. In Makunda's
analysis, that would make Lincoln "massively unfiltered." This
explains his success. Lincoln had little experience but produced
extraordinary results.

In 2016, there are many candidates in the primaries. Some have
relevant political and executive experience. Some are "unfiltered."
It will be difficult to predict who will be the most successful
President under the best of circumstances.

Chapter Three: Communicator

Words are singularly the most powerful force available to humanity. We can choose to use this force constructively with words of encouragement, or destructively using words of despair. Words have energy and power with the ability to help, to heal, to hinder, to hurt, to harm, to humiliate and to humble. **Yehuda Berg**

Whatever words we utter should be chosen with care for people will hear them and be influenced by them for good or ill. **Buddha**

Speak clearly, if you speak at all; carve every word before you let it fall. **Oliver Wendell Holmes, Sr.**

The constant free flow of communication...enabling the free interchange of ideas, forms the very bloodstream of our nation. It keeps the mind and body of our democracy eternally vital, eternally young. **Franklin D. Roosevelt**

I won a nickname, "The Great Communicator." But I never thought it was my style or the words I used that made a difference: It was the content. I wasn't a great communicator, but I communicated great things, and they didn't spring full bloom from my brow, they came from the heart of a great nation -- from our experience, our wisdom, and our belief in principles that have guided us for two centuries. **Ronald Reagan**

You can fool all the people some of the time, and some of the people all the time, but you cannot fool all the people all the time.

Abraham Lincoln

At the heart of Presidential leadership is the ability to communicate. It can take many forms. In the modern era, "tweeting," and other forms of social media and television have become the "bully pulpit" for American Chief Executives to transmit their messages, their vision for the future and to sway political and public opinion. Several have done it supremely well.

Abraham Lincoln delivering the Gettysburg Address, November 19th, 1863, Courtesy the Library of Congress

Fourscore and seven years ago our fathers brought forth on this continent, a new nation, conceived in Liberty, and dedicated to the proposition that all men are created equal...

That this nation, under God, shall have a new birth of freedom – and that government of the people, by the people, for the people, shall not perish from the Earth. **Gettysburg Address**

With malice toward none, with charity for all, with firmness in the right as God gives us to see the right, let us strive on to finish the work we are in, to bind up the nation's wounds, to care for him

who shall have borne the battle and for his widow and his orphan, to do all which may achieve and cherish a just and lasting peace among ourselves and with all nations.

Second Inaugural Address

Abraham Lincoln: The Gettysburg Address and the Second Inaugural Address

Lincoln could write and deliver a short, yet powerful speech. The Gettysburg Address is 2 minutes long. It is an amazing example of verbal compression. His words, phrases and sentences are succinct with few adjectives and no flowery expressions. Historians still study the 270 word talk to find subtle ideas and concepts that continue to be meaningful over 150 years after it was delivered. Such is the case with Lincoln's last speech, his Second Inaugural Address.

A review of Ronald C. White's remarkable book, (*Lincoln's Greatest Speech: The Second Inaugural,* (Simon & Schuster, New York, 2002) described the setting as Abraham Lincoln spoke:

"After four years of unspeakable horror and sacrifice on both sides, the Civil War was about to end. On March 4th, 1865, at his second inauguration, President Lincoln did not offer the North the victory speech it yearned for, nor did he blame the South solely for the sin of slavery. Calling the whole nation to account, Lincoln offered a moral framework for peace and reconciliation. The speech was greeted with indifference, misunderstanding, and hostility by many in the Union. But it was a great work, the victorious culmination of Lincoln's own lifelong struggle with the issue of slavery, and he well understood it to be his most profound speech. Eventually this 'with malice toward none' address would be accepted and revered as one of the greatest in the nation's history...These words, delivered only weeks before his assassination, were the culmination of Lincoln's moral and rhetorical genius."

Lincoln delivering his Second Inaugural Address, Courtesy National Archives

White described it as Lincoln's "Sermon on the Mount." He said, "In the Sermon on the Mount, Jesus offered a new ethic rooted in humility and compassion: 'blessed are those' who do not follow the way of the world — judgment — but follows the new way of grace and mercy. In the Second Inaugural, Lincoln offered a surprising ethic of judgment and reconciliation."

The speech was the second shortest inaugural address in US history. It was 701 words. He spoke for only six or seven minutes. It was more like a homily than a discourse. In his words he articulated the parameters of winning the peace through reconciliation. The true test of whether or not the Civil War was fought for a just cause would be the way we treated those who had been vanquished. Hatred had to end. If not, than the savagery and sacrifice would have been to no avail. "The words were practical as well as beautiful. In this final paragraph, Lincoln offered the ultimate surprise. Instead of rallying his supporters, in the name of God, to support the war, he asked his listeners, quietly, to imitate the ways of God."[45]

Forty one days after he delivered the greatest inaugural address in American history, Abraham Lincoln was dead.

My favorite thought about Abraham Lincoln is he believed in two things: loving one another and working together to make this world better. **Mario Cuomo**

---

[45] Ronald C. White, Jr., *Lincoln's Greatest Speech: The Second Inaugural,* Introduction. (Simon & Schuster, 2002), as reviewed by David Herbert Donald.

"The Great Communicator," Courtesy Reagan Presidential Library

We can't help everyone, but everyone can help someone.

Freedom is never more than one generation away from extinction. We didn't pass it to our children in the bloodstream. It must be fought for, protected, and handed on for them to do the same.

There are no constraints on the human mind, no walls around the human spirit, and no barriers to our progress except those we ourselves erect. **Ronald Reagan**

Ronald Reagan: The Great Communicator

He was called "The Great Communicator." The New York Daily News described him this way:[46]

More than most presidents, Reagan's success was tied directly to his ability not just to speak to the American people, but to communicate with them...but his reputation as The Great Communicator boils down to three basic traits: he was simple; he was clear; he was sincere.

Ronald Reagan had strong beliefs and he shared them in his messages and speeches. He believed in an America that was strong yet compassionate, courageous and just, hardworking and fair. His were the core values of those who grew up in the Great Depression and took care of each other. His were the values of the "Greatest Generation" who fought in World War II to liberate the world from tyranny. His style of speaking was simple and clear: his speeches were no longer than 20 minutes and began by saying what he would say and then say it. [47]

And Ronald Reagan ascended to the moral high ground when he stood in front of the Berlin Wall and challenged his Soviet counterpart, declaring, General Secretary Gorbachev, if you seek peace, if you seek prosperity for the Soviet Union and Eastern Europe, if you seek liberalization: Come here to this gate! Mr. Gorbachev, open this gate! Mr. Gorbachev, tear down this wall!

Reagan's ability to communicate was a reflection of the inner person. He believed that as an American he was living in the greatest country on earth and that it was each person's responsibility to be concerned about the welfare of their fellow man and woman. He was once asked what he viewed as his greatest achievement. The response defined him well.

He said that in the 1920s he was a life guard. In the span of seven

---

[46] Fred Thompson, The New York Daily News, February 11th, 2011, What made Ronald Reagan the Great Communicator: Former U.S. Senator Fred Thompson reflects. http://www.nydailynews.com/opinion/made-ronald-reagan-great-communicator-u-s-senator-fred-thompson-reflects-article-1.133489#ixzz2sZQcziVW

[47] Ibid

summers he saved 77 lives. He considered that his greatest accomplishment.[48]

President John F. Kennedy, Courtesy Library of Congress

As we express our gratitude, we must never forget that the highest appreciation is not to utter words, but to live by them.

Change is the law of life. And those who look only to the past or present are certain to miss the future.

Let every nation know, whether it wishes us well or ill, that we shall pay any price, bear any burden, meet any hardship, support any friend, oppose any foe to assure the survival and the success of liberty.

---

[48] NPR, The Life of Ronald Reagan, A TimeLine, September 18th, 2015, **(1926** Reagan begins work as a lifeguard at Lowell Park, near Dixon. He was credited with saving 77 lives during the seven summers he worked there) http://www.npr.org/news/specials/obits/reagan/timeline.html

My fellow Americans, ask not what your country can do for you, ask what you can do for your country. **John F. Kennedy**

John F. Kennedy: The Berlin Wall

John F. Kennedy delivering his speech at the Berlin Wall, Courtesy National Archives

John Kennedy combined personal charisma with ability to articulate ideas and transmit them with grace, charm and strong oratorical skills. In *Profile of an Orator: John F. Kennedy,* Brian Leggett described JFK's skill this way:[49]

Unlike Ronald Reagan or Margaret Thatcher who were conviction speakers with ideological messages, John Kennedy's platform was more inspiring, pragmatic and liberal. His Inaugural Address and his speech at the Berlin Wall are examples of this. He was a man of his time, and his style suited this epoch of the mass media. Following the dull post war years of the Eisenhower administration, he

---

[49] Brian Leggett, *Profile of an Orator: John F. Kennedy,* April 4th, 2012, IESE Business School Journal in Spain, (http://blog.iese.edu/leggett/2012/04/12/profile-of-an-orator-john-f-kennedy/

brought a new spirit to the body politic. Kennedy's attractive non-verbal style did much to endear him to his audiences.

It was a windy and chilly day in Berlin. It was June, 1963. President John Kennedy rose to speak. A multitude was waiting to hear his words. They would prove to be memorable and historic:

Freedom is indivisible, and when one man is enslaved, all are not free. When all are free, then we look — can look forward to that day when this city will be joined as one and this country and this great Continent of Europe in a peaceful and hopeful globe. When that day finally comes, as it will, the people of West Berlin can take sober satisfaction in the fact that they were in the front lines for almost two decades.

… All free men, wherever they may live, are citizens of Berlin. And, therefore, as a free man, I take pride in the words "Ich bin ein Berliner."

John Kennedy had the talent to communicate a feeling that few of his generation could convey to a new generation of young people: hope. JFK's vision was not tangible. Kennedy was able to convey feeling, understanding and a sense that nothing was impossible.

President Franklin Delano Roosevelt, Courtesy Franklin Roosevelt Presidential Library

2016 Selecting the President

The only thing we have to fear is fear itself

Human kindness has never weakened the stamina or softened the fiber of a free people. A nation does not have to be cruel to be tough.

Yesterday, December seventh, 1941, a date which will live in infamy, the United States of America was suddenly and deliberately attacked by naval and air forces of the Empire of Japan. We will gain the inevitable triumph, so help us God.

*In the future days which we seek to make secure, we look forward to a world founded upon **four essential human freedoms**. The first is **freedom of speech and expression** — everywhere in the world. The second is freedom of every person to worship God in his own way — everywhere in the world. The third is **freedom from want**, which, translated into world terms, means economic understandings which will secure to every nation a healthy peacetime life for its inhabitants — everywhere in the world. The **fourth is freedom from fear**, which, translated into world terms, means a world-wide reduction of armaments to such a point and in such a thorough fashion that no nation will be in a position to commit an act of physical aggression against any neighbor — anywhere in the world. That is no vision of a distant millennium. It is a definite basis for a kind of world attainable in our own time and generation.*

There is a mysterious cycle in human events. To some generations much is given. Of other generations much is expected. This generation of Americans has a rendezvous with destiny. FDR

Franklin Delano Roosevelt: The Fireside Chats

When Franklin Roosevelt was inaugurated President in March, 1933 he inherited from Herbert Hoover a nation that was facing the greatest economic downturn in US history. The Great Depression became a global calamity that spread around the world. Millions of people lost their jobs, thousands of businesses and institutions disappeared. Roosevelt knew that the people needed hope. They needed to be told that the government would take action to meet their needs. The means he would use was the radio.

Radio was growing in popularity and nearly every American home had one by 1933. It allowed people to use their imaginations as they listened. They could create their own images and ideas from the voices, the music and sounds. This was a perfect medium for Franklin Delano Roosevelt. His distinctive voice, his natural optimism and control flowed over the airwaves into homes with his "Fireside Chats." No one could see his disability. All they could do was concentrate on his words, his ideas and the feelings he conveyed.

President Franklin D. Roosevelt delivered his first fireside chat, on the banking crisis, eight days after taking office on March 12, 1933. Courtesy Library of Congress

His broadcasts helped shape American history as never before. He was able to win the hearts and minds of the voting public to support his programs. His speeches helped pass and implement the New Deal. They helped harness the energy of the country to deal with the economic and social problems the nation faced. His "Day of Infamy" speech on December 8th, 1941, asking for a declaration of war against Japan served to unite the nation behind the government to bring the United States to victory.

2016 requires a Commander and Chief who is a splendid communicator to articulate the solutions to our problems and earn trust, respect and support from the people and the Congress. He or she needs to know the importance and proper use of social media to convey messages solicit feedback and broaden and deepen the process of democratic inclusion so that more people comprehend our collective stake in a successful Presidency.

We must get the American public to look past the glitter, beyond the showmanship, to the reality, the hard substance of things. And we'll do it not so much with speeches that will bring people to their feet as with speeches that bring people to their senses.

Mario Cuomo

Chapter Four: The Brain Trust and the Understanding of Collaboration

Teamwork makes the dream work, but a vision becomes a nightmare when the leader has a big dream and a bad team. **John C. Maxwell**

Talent wins games, but teamwork and intelligence wins championships. **Michael Jordan**

You can talk about teamwork on a baseball team, but I'll tell you, it takes teamwork when you have 2,900 men stationed on the U.S.S. Alabama in the South Pacific. **Bob Feller**

Unity is strength... when there is teamwork and collaboration, wonderful things can be achieved. **Mattie Stepanek**

We should seek by all means in our power to avoid war, by analyzing possible causes, by trying to remove them, by discussion in a spirit of collaboration and good will. **Neville Chamberlain**

America still has the right stuff to thrive. We still have the most creative, diverse, innovative culture and open society - in a world where the ability to imagine and generate new ideas with speed and to implement them through global collaboration is the most important competitive advantage. **Thomas Friedman**

The only thing that will redeem mankind is cooperation. **Bertrand Russell**

The ability of a President to succeed in tackling the enormous challenges that face our country depends on the people they bring into the government to govern with them and their ability to collaborate with them to get the job done and, of great importance, their skill in working with the Congress. They cannot do it alone. Thousands of political appointees must be selected, cleared, approved by the Senate and put into place to oversee the vast bureaucracy of the American government. Our most successful Presidents have brought with them a "Brain Trust" of talent to help them lead. They worked closely with them to achieve their objectives.

President Barack Obama with his cabinet, November, 2009, Courtesy the White House

The President of the United States confronts a wide range of issues that no Chief Executive of any country deals with. The President must also be able to work with international leaders on a whole range of issues from war to peace, from the environment to terrorism and epidemics that cross global boundaries.

Among the President's most critical decisions is the formation of a team that will help them make the transition from candidate to President and who will head the various cabinet agencies:

The President's Cabinet

The Cabinet is the President's team. The Secretaries of each Department and the heads of each Agency administer the apparatus of the government. They also transmit the philosophy of the new Administration. The policies, plans and principles and laws that the President wants to put into effect, with the approval of the Congress, flow through the bureaucracy administered by the Cabinet. Under each Department and Agency head are scores of offices with specific functions managed by political appointees selected by the President and his team. They must reflect the principles of the President as well as exhibit important leadership qualities to do their job. They take the same oath as the President of the United States and swear to protect and defend the Constitution of the United States. It is essential that those appointed and selected for high political offices be people of integrity, skill and trust. This is why we say: "When we elect a President we elect a Government."

The Cabinet of the President of the United States consists of:

The Vice-President
Secretary of State
Secretary of Treasury
Secretary of Defense
Attorney General (Justice Department Head)
Secretary of Interior
Secretary of Agriculture
Secretary of Commerce
Secretary of Labor
Secretary of Health & Human Services
Secretary of Housing & Urban Development
Secretary of Transportation
Secretary of Energy

Secretary of Education
Secretary of Veteran Affairs
Chief of Staff of the White House
Director of the Office of Management & Budget
Legal Counselor to the President
U.S. Trade Representative

FDR's Brain Trust

Franklin D. Roosevelt's 1933 Brains Trust

Adolf Berle
(1895-1971)

Raymond Moley
(1886-1975)

Rexford Tugwell
(1891-1979)

Courtesy Armstrong Economics http://www.armstrongeconomics.com/research/economic-thought/economics/roosevelts-brains-trust

On November 13th, 2008, a week after Barak Obama was elected President, Time Magazine did a study to examine the 10 best Cabinet Members in the 20th Century. 4 of the 10 were members of Franklin Roosevelt's Cabinet.[50]

The first 100 days of the Roosevelt administration were characterized by a whirlwind of activity by a group of advisers to the President known as the "Brain Trust."

---

[50] Time, November 13th, 2008, Top Ten Best Cabinet Members,
http://content.time.com/time/specials/packages/completelist/0,29569,1858368,00.html

"Looks as if the new Leadership was really going to lead." March 7th, 1933, by Ray of the Kansas City Star.

They were charged with taking action to solve the nation's severe economic problems and prepare legislation that would move the arm of government to deal with the poverty and pessimism of the Great Depression. FDR asked for emergency powers from the Congress and immediately set about using them. One of his first acts was to declare a bank holiday which shut down every bank in the country to stop depositors from withdrawing their money. It ended the panic. The largest volume of legislation in US history was passed in a matter of months. By 1938, the Franklin Roosevelt transformed the American economy in a way that no one before or after him has done. [51]

---

[51] The Gilder Lehrman Institute of American History, New Deal Legislation.

New Deal Legislation

1932	Reconstruction Finance Corporation	Granted emergency loans to banks, life insurance companies, and railroads
1933	Civilian Conservation Corps (CCC)	Employed youth in reforestation, road construction, and flood control projects
	Agricultural Adjustment Act	Direct payments to farmers to reduce production
	Tennessee Valley Authority (TVA)	Creates independent public corporation to construct dams and power projects
	National Industrial Recovery Act	Establishes fair-competition codes; section 7a guarantees labor's right to organize Public Works Administration Public works
1934	Federal Housing Administration (FHA)	Insured home loans
1935	Works Progress Administration (WPA)	Employed 8 million on public works projects
	Social Security Act	Established unemployment compensation and old age insurance
	National Labor Relations Act	Creates National Labor Relations Board to prevent unfair labor Practices
1937	National Housing Act	Authorizes low rent public housing projects
1938	Fair Labor Standards Act	minimum wage of 40 cts/hr and 40 hour work week

The Cabinet of President Franklin Roosevelt, 1933, Courtesy the Library of Congress

Roosevelt appointed a cabinet that was skilled politically, economically and socially. It included the first woman, Francis Perkins, as Secretary of Labor. FDR relied on his Brain Trust of advisers to help create new laws and work legislation through Congress. His Cabinet ran the bureaucracy, interfaced with the House and the Senate and the many constituencies in business, labor and farming. He relied on Francis Perkins and Eleanor Roosevelt to stay in close touch with social groups throughout the nation to better understand and meet the needs of the people. In a

111

review of Ken Burn's PBS Documentary, "The Roosevelts," Professor Peter Drier says:[52]

Burns and his interviewees describe FDR as courageous, bold, supremely self-confident, optimistic, not rigidly ideological, open to new ideas and willing to experiment. In his actions and speeches (including his popular fireside chats on the radio), FDR gave Americans confidence in themselves and reminded them that the national government could be a positive force in their daily lives.

But missing from The Roosevelts is the real secret of FDR's success - the escalating protests that created a sense of urgency throughout the country and the political savvy of a small cadre of FDR's progressive advisors.

FDR may not have ended the Great Depression. Yet, he provided hope and strength to the people of America that they could continue to grow and develop even during difficult times. He also helped create stronger alliances between industry, labor and agriculture through "priming the pump" to increase consumption, legislation supporting workers' rights and helping farmers rise up from the Dust Bowl.

Ray, the Kansas City Star, 1937

This coalition and the economic resiliency created by the New Deal was the foundation of the generation FDR prepared to confront America's greatest challenge: World War II.

---

[52] Peter Drier, George Mason University, "Ken Burns Overlooks the Secret of FDR's Success: The Power of the People, HNN History News Network, and September 28th, 2014. http://historynewsnetwork.org/article/157061

Saint-Memin sketched this last portrait of Washington in Philadelphia in November 1799. (John Hill Morgan, *Life Portraits of George Washington and Their Replicas* [1931].)

If the freedom of speech is taken away then dumb and silent we may be led, like sheep to the slaughter.

The Constitution is the guide which I never will abandon.

Observe good faith and justice toward all nations. Cultivate peace and harmony with all....To be prepared for war is one of the most effective means of preserving peace.

I hope I shall possess firmness and virtue enough to maintain what I consider the most enviable of all titles, the character of an honest man.

My first wish is to see this plague of mankind, war, banished from the earth. **George Washington**

George Washington and the first "Team of Rivals"[53]

When Washington assumed the office of the President on April 30th, 1789, he found a nation that had serious financial problems and, most of all, did not have the ability to carry out the principles embodied in the Bill of Rights and the Constitution. It was his task to create the first government of the United States of America.

Washington picked men of great courage and skill to be his advisers and the members of his Cabinet. There were four (there are 16 today): Thomas Jefferson, Secretary of State, Alexander Hamilton, Secretary of Treasury, Henry Knox, Attorney General and Edmond Randolph, Attorney General. He trusted them and relied on them to help him construct the new republic on strong democratic principles.

Washington proved to be a wise and pragmatic visionary. He understood human nature. He knew that Hamilton and Jefferson were serious political and philosophical rivals. Jefferson felt he represented the common man. Hamilton believed in the merchant and aristocracy. Washington needed their brilliance to help him run the nascent government. He was sufficiently confident in himself to preside over their disputes, keep them in check and delay the beginning of party warfare.

He needed time to set his house in order and, in the process, stay out of Europe's deadly quarrels. He felt that America needed at least three decades of peace and prosperity before it could resist any aggression from foreign powers. He was right.

After eight years in office, he proved to be a splendid administrator. He held regular Cabinet meetings. He allowed his team to debate but left the final decisions for himself. He followed up to make sure

---

[53] In reference to the book, Team of Rivals, by Doris Kearns Goodwin, Simon and Shuster, New York, 2005

they were implemented. He knew how to delegate, control and command. He was a superb judge of character and talent.

Washington and his "Brain Trust 'organized the Executive Branch; established the federal judiciary; helped amend the Constitution; established the location of the nation's capital; created the first bank of the United States; established the dollar as the medium of exchange among the 13 states; started the US Navy and signed treaties of friendship with other countries. Washington's influence lasted for decades and helped produce the foundation of the country we know today and our values.

Lincoln presented the Emancipation Proclamation to his Cabinet on July 22, 1862. Shown from left to right are: Edwin M. Stanton, Secretary of War (seated); Salmon P. Chase, Secretary of the Treasury (standing);Abraham Lincoln; Gideon Welles, Secretary of the Navy (seated);Caleb Blood Smith, Secretary of the Interior (standing);William H. Seward, Secretary of State (seated);Montgomery Blair, Postmaster General (standing);Edward Bates, Attorney General (seated). Courtesy US Senate

We need the strongest men of the party in the Cabinet. We needed to hold our people together. I had looked the party over and

concluded that these were the very strongest men. Then I had no right to deprive the country of their services. Abraham Lincoln

Mr. Lincoln's Cabinet

No President encountered the trials of Abraham Lincoln. He entered the Presidency with an empty treasury and with a country divided by slavery that threatened the existence of the United States. He needed the best talent to help him. Lincoln did not care if the members of his Cabinet liked him or he liked them. They had the most serious task before them: save the Union. This was his goal and he required strong leaders to run the agencies. Even if they disagreed with each other and even if they disagreed with him, in the, it was Lincoln who made the decisions. It was Lincoln who bore the awesome burden of responsibility.

1860 Republican Party Presidential Candidates, Courtesy National Archives

All of his chief rivals for the Republican nomination for President in 1860 were part of his Cabinet: William H. Seward, Salmon P. Chase, Simon Cameron and Edward Bates. The selection involved considerable conflict. Some were promised jobs as part of the deal to support Lincoln's nomination. Several objected to the inclusion of their rivals in the Cabinet. Differences arose about geographic distribution of jobs; balance between former members of the Democratic and Whig parties; disagreement about ideology, personality and ethics. Cameron, for example, was attacked for his reputation of shady political and financial transactions.

Lincoln saw value in his team. For example, Seward, as Secretary of State, could be depended on to keep close ties with the British and the French to avoid having them take sides in the Civil War. Secretary of War Stanton was tough and determined and resilient especially in the early years of the war that were difficult for the North. Chase, as Secretary of the Treasury, was charged with financing the war effort. He worked with Lincoln to create the greenback, which was the US's first universal paper currency, and found ways to raise funds to help win the conflict.

The members of Lincoln's Cabinet were fiercely independent, opinionated and prone to constant conflict. They had one overriding factor in common: they were appointed by Abraham Lincoln. They respected him and his authority, even though this did not always seem the case. Lincoln was supremely confident in his own ability to make wise choices after he listened to the opinions of his advisers. During Cabinet sessions and individual meetings with Cabinet officers, he would patiently concentrate on the discussion at hand, allow everyone their say and then he would decide. He was never in a hurry or showed impatience. He was constantly cordial and pleasant to everyone. He rarely revealed his thoughts until he definitely made up his mind. At that point, it was clear that the last word was that of Abraham Lincoln.

Lincoln showed remarkable courage and wisdom in selecting a "team of rivals" for his Cabinet. If he had done it otherwise, the outcome of the Civil War might have been different.

Abraham Lincoln also created the benchmarks of the modern Presidency. His was the role model. His high character, integrity, perseverance and wisdom unquestionably demonstrated that a President could succeed by being virtuous as well as skillful, focused and determined to succeed.

A case where a President needed a strong "Brain Trust" and Cabinet to help him and a powerful international coalition to deal with an international crisis was when George H.W. Bush had to confront the challenge of the Iraqi invasion of Kuwait in 1990.

A new breeze is blowing, and a world refreshed by freedom seems reborn; for in man's heart, if not in fact, the day of the dictator is over. The totalitarian era is passing, its old ideas blown away like leaves from an ancient, lifeless tree.

We don't want an America that is closed to the world. What we want is a world that is open to America.

I can tell you this: If I'm ever in a position to call the shots, I'm not going to rush to send somebody else's kids into a war.

One of the good things about the way the Gulf War ended in 1991 is, you'd see the Vietnam veterans marching with the Gulf War veterans. **George H. W. Bush**

George H. W. Bush announcing the start of the first Gulf War, January 16th, 1991, Courtesy George Herbert Walker Bush Presidential Library

George H. W. Bush's International Coalition in the Gulf War

"Just 2 hours ago, allied air forces began an attack on military targets in Iraq and Kuwait. These attacks continue as I speak. Ground forces are not engaged.

This conflict started August 2nd when the dictator of Iraq invaded a small and helpless neighbor. Kuwait -- a member of the Arab League and a member of the United Nations -- was crushed; its people, brutalized. Five months ago, Saddam Hussein started this cruel war against Kuwait. Tonight, the battle has been joined."[54]

With these words, President George Bush announced the start of the battle to liberate Kuwait from the grip of Saddam Hussein. Five months earlier, Iraq invaded Kuwait. The aggression sent shock

---

[54] The History Place, Great Speeches Collection, G.H.W. Bush Announcing War Against Iraq, http://www.historyplace.com/speeches/bush-war.htm

waves around the world. President George H.W. Bush saw the attack as a threat to the economic and global political interests of the United States. It was a threat to the oil states in the Gulf and it was a direct threat to the international system that was evolving after the end of the Cold War. Bush believed that reversing the conquest of Kuwait would help create a "new world order" to prevent this kind of action happening in the future. He equated the invasion in terms of "good and evil," comparing Saddam Hussein to Adolf Hitler.

Coalition forces from France, Kuwait, Syria, Oman and Egypt assemble during Operation Desert Storm, Courtesy US. Department of the Navy

Within hours the United Nations Security Council passed the first of twelve resolutions condemning Iraq and imposing sanctions. Even the Soviet Union stood by the US. It condemned the invasion and halted arm sales to Iraq. The United States assembled a coalition of forces that participated in the war to liberate Kuwait.

The President was directly involved in planning the war effort. He wanted a clear cut victory that was quick and decisive and left no room for defeat. A day after the President's speech, allied and American forces started air attacks on Iraqi forces. Thirty-seven days later the ground campaign began. Exactly one hundreds hours after the start of the campaign the coalition announced "mission accomplished." Iraqi forces were driven out of Kuwait.

The day will come - and it is not far off - when the legacy of Lincoln will finally be fulfilled at 1600 Pennsylvania Avenue, when a black man or woman will sit in the Oval Office. When that day comes, the most remarkable thing about it will be how naturally it occurs.
George H. W. Bush

The Ability to Work with the Congress

I don't make jokes. I just watch the government and report the facts.

Ancient Rome declined because it had a Senate, now what's going to happen to us with both a House and a Senate?

I am not a member of any organized political party. I am a Democrat. **Will Rogers**

The Congress can be an ally or an enemy to a new Administration. It is up to the President to have the skill, patience and wherewithal to understand how to work closely with the House and the Senate. Our most effective Presidents have been able to deal with Congress even when both houses were in opposition. Several Presidents enjoyed majorities in the Congress which gave them significant opportunities to change the course of events. For example, in the last century three Chief Executives stand out in their ability to control and sway the Congress and pass important legislation: Woodrow Wilson, Franklin Roosevelt and Lyndon Johnson

Woodrow Wilson being sworn in on March 4th, 1913, Courtesy Library of Congress

Woodrow Wilson's "New Freedom"

Woodrow Wilson entered the Presidency in 1913 with a strong sense of purpose and aggressiveness. [55] He believed the Presidency was a place "in which a man must put on war paint." Wilson was bold and willing to gamble for great stakes in order to achieve his goals. He approached politics this way from winning the governorship of New Jersey in 1911 to his victory to become the 28th President of the United States two years later. He had defeated

---

[55] August *Heckscher*, (1991). Woodrow Wilson. Easton Press, pp. 265-267

2016 Selecting the President

the incumbent Republican President, William Howard Taft and one of the most popular politicians in American history, Theodore Roosevelt, in a three party race.

Wilson was the first Southerner elected to the Presidency since 1869. He campaigned as a reformer and advocate of control over big business and political patronage. He enjoyed a Democratic majority in the Congress. As a college professor, Wilson had studied and written about politics, the party system and the Congress. He was a keen student of how the apparatus worked and used his knowledge to push his "New Freedom" program to create the Federal Reserve, the Federal Trade Commission, the enactment of a progressive income tax and stronger anti-trust measures. He skillfully manipulated the Democratic caucus to carefully coordinate with Congressional leaders the introduction and passage of legislation. Often times, Republicans were kept out of conference committee deliberations and left out of the legislative process. "Never did the lash of the presidential and caucus whip cut so deep as today," one Republican complained.[56]

By the end of World War I, in 1918, the legislative situation had changed. The Senate was now in the hands of the Republicans. They remembered Wilson's style of ramming through laws with little or no consultation. Wilson did not invite members of the opposition to join him at the Paris Peace Conference in Versailles. The Republicans did not forget this. When he returned from the Conference, Wilson wanted the Senate to accept the League of Nations. He refused to compromise even when the Republicans introduced amendments that were deemed acceptable. The proposal was defeated. It was an historic mistake on the part of the

---

[56] How presidents work Congress by Julian E. Zelizer, Politico, July 27th, 2009
http://www.politico.com/story/2009/07/how-presidents-work-congress-025441#ixzz3qzAyXNTM

Executive and Legislative branches of our government. Historians claim that if the US had been an active member of the League many of the events leading up to World War II could have been avoided.

The question of the League and the comportment of Woodrow Wilson during the Paris Peace Conference brings into question a serious issue about the US Presidency: the health of the President. The first ominous signs of Wilson's serious health issues showed up in the summer of 1918 when the President began to suffer from severe breathing problems. The issue was hushed up but was the prelude to more critical problems to come. Historian John Milton Cooper, a Wilson scholar at the University of Wisconsin, in his 2001 book, *Breaking the Heart of the World: Woodrow Wilson and the Fight for the League of Nations*, claimed that Wilson was not well in Paris. He was under considerable psychological and physical stress, so much so that it may have affected his ability to negotiate and come to grips with the realities of the post war period in Europe. [57] Returning to America, Wilson set out on a demanding public speaking tour to gain support for ratification of the Treaty of Versailles and the proposal for American acceptance of the League of Nations. On September 25th, 1919, the President collapsed while in Pueblo, Colorado. He never fully recovered. Two weeks later he suffered a serious stroke. Wilson was paralyzed on the left side and partially blind. He remained bed ridden for weeks. His wife arranged for him to have absolute privacy and keep his condition from reaching the public until February, 1920 when it became known. He remained in seclusion for the rest of his time in office. "This is the worst instance of presidential disability we've ever had," according to Cooper, a. "We stumbled along . . . without a

---

[57] John Milton Cooper, *Breaking the Heart of the World, Woodrow Wilson and the Fight for the League of Nations*, 2001 by Cambridge University Press, London.

fully functioning President" for a year and a half, he said. [58]
Woodrow Wilson died on February 3rd, 1924 at the age of sixty-seven.

Wilson's fitness for the Presidency was questioned during and after his time in office. It became an issue that was part of the motivation to pass the 25th Amendment to the Constitution in 1967 that dealt with the succession to the Presidency if the incumbent was unable to discharge his or her duties or resigned.

FDR and the Congress

It IS a New Deal

It IS a New Deal, March 11th, 1933, by Talburt in the Pittsburgh Press, Courtesy FDR Library

---

[58] Michael Alison Chandler, A President's Illness Kept Under Wraps, Washington Post Staff Writer. Saturday, February 3, 2007

The election of 1932 brought Franklin Roosevelt and a majority of Democrats to the Congress. He got 57% of the vote while his Party went from 50% of the seats in the House of Representatives to 72%. The Democrats also dominated the Senate with 59 Senators. Two years later, his majority grew. It was the election of 1934 that gave FDR the Congress he needed to enact most of the legislation of the New Deal.

FDR seemed unstoppable. He dominated the Congress and its activities during his first term and with the landslide election of 1934, he placed his party in a dominant position for the first time since the 1850s. Roosevelt campaigned extensively for congressional candidates. Many owed their careers to him. With his massive re-election mandate of 1936, Roosevelt and the Congress believed that the people wanted to continue the policies of the New Deal to re-engineer the economic and social conditions of America.

"During his first two terms, FDR oversaw some of the most far-reaching economic and social legislation in the nation's history, including Social Security, protections of workers' rights to unionize, a federal minimum wage, heavier taxes on the wealthy, new regulations on banks, public utilities and business stock transactions, a huge work relief program for the unemployed and unemployment insurance. Several government-sponsored enterprises brought electricity and jobs to rural areas, including the Tennessee Valley Authority. The Civilian Conservation Corps put 300,000 young men to work in 1,200 camps planting trees, building bridges and cleaning beaches. The Public Works Administration (PWA), and later the Works Progress Administration (WPA), provided jobs to millions of Americans to build schools, libraries, hospitals, airports and roads. It also paid artists, writers, actors and others to create murals, produce plays and musicals, and write travel guides and oral histories." [59] The alliance of FDR and the Congress changed the face of the United States forever.

Lyndon Baines Johnson: Man of the Congress

Lyndon Baines Johnson, 1964, Courtesy National Archives

The Democratic Party won seven out of nine Presidential elections from 1932 to 1964. During those three decades they enjoyed almost a continuous majority in the Congress. Lyndon Johnson rose in the ranks of the Party beginning in the second administration of FDR.

---

[59] Peter Dreier, Truthout, "Ken Burns Overlooks Secret of FDR's Success: Power of the People," Friday, 26 September 2014 10:48 By | News Analysis

He became a member of the House in 1937 and served until 1949 when he was elected Senator from his home state of Texas. For the next dozen years Johnson rose in the ranks to become one of the most powerful Senate majority leaders in history. He was sworn in as Vice President in 1961 and became President with the assassination of John F. Kennedy. The distinguishing characteristic of Johnson that separated him from other Presidents was his profound roots in the Congress. After serving more than 20 years he became an expert in moving legislation through both houses. He could cajole or intimidate and convince his colleagues to support his positions. He was resourceful but also willing to compromise. He carried this skill into the White House.

LBJ was elected in 1964 with over 61% of the vote which was the highest share up to that time. The Democrats won the largest majorities in Congress since FDR's election of 1936. Johnson set about passing the program advocated by John Kennedy and creating welfare legislation for what he coined, "The War on Poverty." Thanks to his strong control of the legislative branch he was able to pass a flurry of laws that were comparable to those of the New Deal in terms of impact on society and the economy. They included:

- 1963 Clean Air Act of 1963
- 1963: Higher Education Facilities Act of 1963
- 1963: Vocational Education Act of 1963
- 1964: Civil Rights Act of 1964
- 1964: Urban Mass Transportation Act of 1964
- 1964: Wilderness Act
- 1964: Nurse Training Act of 1964
- 1964: Food Stamp Act of 1964
- 1964: Economic Opportunity Act
- 1964: Housing Act of 1964[262]
- 1965: Higher Education Act of 1965
- 1965: Older Americans Act
- 1965: Coinage Act of 1965

- ☐ 1965: Social Security Act of 1965
- ☐ 1965: Voting Rights Act
- ☐ 1965: Immigration and Nationality Services Act of 1965
- ☐ 1966: Animal Welfare Act of 1966
- ☐ 1966: Freedom of Information Act (FOIA)
- ☐ 1967: Age Discrimination in Employment Act
- ☐ 1967: Public Broadcasting Act of 1967
- ☐ 1968: Architectural Barriers Act of 1968
- ☐ 1968: Bilingual Education Act
- ☐ 1968: Civil Rights Act of 1968
- ☐ 1968: Gun Control Act of 1968

Even the development of the FCC emergency number 911, was created during the Johnson Administration.

The same Congress that helped Lyndon Johnson create "The Great Society," was also responsible for our involvement in Vietnam. Johnson's legacy as President and the legacy of the legislation he passed was summed up by the Miller Center of the University of Virginia:

"Johnson's administration passed an unprecedented amount of legislation, with much of it designed to protect the nation's land, air, water, wilderness, and quality of life—to keep Americans safer and the United States from becoming uglier and dirtier. President Johnson's administration also extended the New Deal of Franklin Roosevelt, including aid to education, Head Start, Medicare, and Medicaid—programs that are still significant today and that command bipartisan support for their effectiveness. But many of his initiatives for the arts, for the environment, for poverty, for racial justice, and for workplace safety angered many economic and social conservatives and became the targets of alienated white voters and tax revolters. The reaction to his Great Society and to broader trends helped spawn a dramatic political polarization in the United States that some historians have labeled a conservative counterrevolution.

Further clouding Johnson's legacy was the devastating outcome of the Vietnam War. While his programs kept untold numbers of Americans out of poverty, gave others basic health care, and ensured the fundamental rights of citizenship for minorities, in Southeast Asia, millions of Vietnamese lost their lives and homes, more than 58,000 American military personnel lost their lives, and hundreds of thousands more would have their lives permanently altered. At a time when Americans were reshaping the locus of power at home, events in Vietnam were raising serious questions about how America should use its clout abroad. The legacies of death, renewal, and opportunity attached to the Johnson administration are ironic, confusing, and uncertain. They will likely remain that way."[60]

Now more than ever we need a President who will be able to identify and convince the best and brightest experts to join the government to tackle the great issues we confront. The "Brain Trust" requires the skill to build and manage a team dedicated to the principles that put them into office and the trust given them by the people of America. Working closely with the Congress is absolutely essential. No President can govern with Executive Orders alone. The next President must also be able to work and collaborate with other nations to seek global peace and stability especially today when we face threats that risk the future of the safety and security of the entire world.

---

[60] Miller Center, University of Virginia, Lyndon B. Johnson: Impact and Legacyhttp://millercenter.org/president/biography/lbjohnson-impact-and-legacy

Chapter Five: Character, integrity, ethical behavior and trustworthiness

Reputation is the shadow. Character is the tree. **Abraham Lincoln**

Goodness is about character - integrity, honesty, kindness, generosity, moral courage, and the like. More than anything else, it is about how we treat other people. **Dennis Prager**

Character cannot be developed in ease and quiet. Only through experience of trial and suffering can the soul be strengthened, ambition inspired, and success achieved. **Helen Keller**

I have a dream that my four little children will one day live in a nation where they will not be judged by the color of their skin, but by the content of their character. **Martin Luther King, Jr.**

Be more concerned with your character than your reputation, because your character is what you really are, while your reputation is merely what others think you are. **John Wooden**

In any moment of decision, the best thing you can do is the right thing, the next best thing is the wrong thing, and the worst thing you can do is nothing....I am really sorry for Taft... I am sure he means well, but he means well feebly, and he does not know how! He is utterly unfit for leadership and this is a time when we need leadership...No man is worth his salt who is not ready at all times to risk his well-being, to risk his body, to risk his life, in a great cause. **Theodore Roosevelt**

Theodore Roosevelt shortly before being shot, October 14th, 1912. Courtesy Library of Congress

The complicated ethical qualities that make up each person and govern the way we react in any given situation are what we know as *Character*. It includes honesty, and ethics, trustworthiness and self-control. It is about always doing the right thing, no matter what.

Someone, for instance, who has a strong character trait of truthfulness and integrity, is more likely to report honestly the facts than one who is prone to being deceptive. Someone who has a very alert character may be a safer pilot than someone who is unable to quickly recognize potential perils. Someone who respects diversity will be more accepting of the different qualities people have. Character which includes integrity and ethical behavior may be the most important quality that a President of the United States should have. Without character a President would not be able to gain the trust of his team, his allies and the people he governs.

President William Howard Taft, Courtesy the White House

I am going to do what I think is best for the country, within my jurisdiction and power, and then let the rest take care of itself.

A man never knows exactly how the child of his brain will strike other people. **William Howard Taft**

Theodore Roosevelt: Attempted Assassination

It was 1912. Republican William Howard Taft was running for re-election. He was up against the Democrat nominee, New Jersey Governor Woodrow Wilson and, one of the most popular men in American history, his former friend and

2016 Selecting the President

mentor, Theodore Roosevelt. Teddy was President from 1901 to 1908. He refused to run for a third term to honor the precedent set by George Washington. He left the White House with soaring popularity as he turned over the reins to Taft. Teddy went off to big game hunting in Africa to bring back specimens for the Smithsonian Institution. He returned 3 years later.

Governor of New York	Vice President	President	Peacemaker	Mighty Hunter all the time

By then, Teddy had become dissatisfied with the performance of his successor. He ran against Taft for the Republican nomination and far outpolled him in the primaries. Taft worked vigorously to control the Party's organizational apparatus which ran the nomination process. The Republican National Convention selected him on June 22nd, 1912 as their standard bearer. Teddy's supporters met the next day to create a third party. In August, 1912, the newly formed Progressive Party convened with great enthusiasm. Jane Adams, the legendary suffragette, gave a strong supporting speech to second the nomination of

Theodore Roosevelt as the candidate for President of the United States of the Progressive Party (reporters coined it the Bull Moose Party in honor of Teddy). He was selected by acclamation. The platform was a detailed document of dramatic social change called "A Contract With the People." The theme was to eliminate the corrupt domination of business interests in politics.

It promised strict limits on campaign contributions, full disclosure of contributions and registration of lobbyists. The Social Platform called for a National Health Service, social insurance to provide for the disabled and elderly, sweeping legislation for workers' rights including a minimum wage for women and an eight hour day. Political reforms emphasized women's suffrage, recall elections, judicial recall, referendums and the direct election of Senators. Teddy carried out a vigorous campaign. He travelled extensively and gave scores of speeches and interviews. He met with people of all political persuasions and explained the principles of the Progressive Party Platform.

Roosevelt mixing spicy ingredients in his speeches in this 1912 editorial cartoon by Karl K. Knecht in the *Evansville Courier,* Courtesy Library of Congress

On October 14th, 1912, he was campaigning in Milwaukee, Wisconsin. It was just after 8 PM when Teddy entered his car outside the Gilpatrick Hotel. He rose and waved his hat to the crowd that gathered to greet him. Suddenly, a light flashed and an explosion lit the night air. A would be assassin had shot Theodore Roosevelt at close range. The bullet lodged against his rib on a path to his heart. It was slowed by an eye glass case and his 50 page speech which he was on his way to give at the Milwaukee Auditorium.

The crowd now became a mob. The coolest head was that of Theodore Roosevelt. The man who entered the White House after the murder of William McKinley bellowed, "Don't hurt him. Bring him here." He asked, "What did you do it for?" The would-be assassin was silent. "Oh, what's the use? Turn him over to the police," said Teddy.

There were no signs of blood on his clothes. Roosevelt reached inside and felt a bullet hole, the size of a dime, on the right side in the lower part of his chest. He coughed three times to see if the bullet had penetrated his lung. It had not. A doctor, accompanying the former President's caravan, ordered the driver to go directly to the nearest hospital. Roosevelt yelled, "No. You get me to that speech."[61]

Roosevelt told the audience he had been shot. The audience gasped. It was a bombshell. He opened his vest and revealed his shirt, soaked in blood. He took out his speech which was filled with bullet holes.

Fortunately I had my manuscript, so you see I was going to make a long speech, and there is a bullet—there is where the bullet went through—and it probably saved me from it going into my heart. The bullet is in me now, so that I cannot make a very long speech, but I will try my best...I have a message to deliver," he declared to the stunned audience, "and I will deliver it as long as there is life in my body." It was a rousing performance. Roosevelt was a wonderful, charismatic orator under any circumstance, and the sight of his spattered shirt and notes added a spectacular portion of drama to his speech.[62]

He continued his speech for 90 minutes. Only then did he agree to go to the hospital. The bullet stayed with him for the rest of his life and exacerbated his chronic rheumatoid arthritis. A few weeks later the votes were cast. Teddy drew over 4 million votes. It was 27% of the total but fell behind Wilson with 42%. Taft got only 23%.[63]

---

[61] David Kerisy and Ray Choiniere, Presidential Temperament: The Unfolding of Character in the Forty Presidents of the United States, University of Toronto Press, Toronto, 1992, Introduction.

[62] Ibid Kerisy and Choiniere.

[63] Congressional Quarterly's Guide to U. S. elections. Washington, DC: Congressional Quarterly Inc. 1985. pp. 75, 387–388, ISBN 0-87187-339-, pp. 295, 348

"More Rough Riding," Teddy trying to dominate the Party, 1912 editorial cartoon by Karl K. Knecht in the *Evansville Courier,* Courtesy Library of Congress

Two Gentlemen, Charles J. Budd, Courtesy Harper's Weekly, November 9th, 1912.

On March 4th, 1913, Woodrow Wilson was sworn in as the 28th President of the United States succeeding William Howard Taft.

President William McKinley, Courtesy Library of Congress

His kindly nature and lovable traits of character, and his amiable consideration for all about him will long live in the minds and hearts of his countrymen. Former President Grover Cleveland on the death of William McKinley

That's all a man can hope for during his lifetime - to set an example - and when he is dead, to be an inspiration for history.

William McKinley

The Altruism of William McKinley

Eleven years before the attempt on Roosevelt's life, President William McKinley was also the victim of a gunman. McKinley was attending an event in Buffalo, New York, on September 6th, 1901 when he was shot by an anarchist. The President died 8 days later. Theodore was sworn in on September 14th, 1901.

The details of McKinley's shooting were almost identical to Roosevelt's: a famous political figure is walking in public; a lone madman steps up and fires a pistol point blank into his chest; the gunman is immediately wrestled to the ground while the bloodied victim, still conscious, sees his assailant subdued. In President McKinley's case, however, the rest of the story is quite different. As the mortally wounded McKinley watched the madman Leon Czolgosz being subdued, he cried out, "Don't let them hurt him!" Then, to his secretary George Cortelyou he gasped, "My wife--be careful, Cortelyou, how you tell her--oh, be careful!" Then as his supporters rushed him to the hospital he sighed, "It must have been some poor misguided fellow." [64]

The reaction of each man to the crisis in question revealed much about their character. Teddy responded like the tough, fierce warrior he had been all his life. William McKinley, instead, while being a dedicated and determined leader, was by nature more considerate and gentle. His first concern was the welfare of his assassin and the impact on his wife. This was typical of McKinley. As was Roosevelt's fiery reaction. Both men reacted to the same event in manners consistent with the way they lived and their character: McKinley was a kind and serious caretaker; Teddy was a spur of the moment, enthusiastic swashbuckler. [65]

We are not suggesting here that social background and personal history are unimportant. Far from it; our social context stamps us inevitably and indelibly. But we feel quite safe in proposing that our life-long patterns of action, our character, will always arise from and be consistent with our temperament. Thus William McKinley and Teddy Roosevelt, each of a different temperament, could never have developed similar characters, similar ways of looking at and responding to the world. They saw differently and they responded differently, quite consistently with their differing temperaments, even to the almost identical traumas of their shootings. [66]

---

[64] Ibid Kerisy and Choiniere.
[65] Ibid Kerisy and Choiniere.
[66] Ibid Kerisy and Choiniere.

Presidential Temperaments

David Kerisy and Ray Choiniere, in their 1992 book, *Presidential Temperament: The Unfolding of Character in the Forty Presidents of the United States,* studied the behavior of forty American Presidents. They found that each acted in an amazing variety of ways. Some were timid; some were vigorous; others were heroic and domineering figures while others seemed immobile. At times, they took on the characteristics of animals. At times they could be lions exhibiting courage and strength; and other times like foxes, acting with cunning and opportunism. They could be playful like dogs or beavers building and protecting their nests or owls, high above all, waiting for a moment worthy of their concentration. [67]

Kerisy and Choiniere explained that four basic temperaments from which character is fashioned: [68]

Guardian:

Are considered "concrete cooperators" who dwell on their responsibilities and duties. They are protectors of what they can control and are careful to follow rules, respect the rights of others and obey laws. Idealists: "Abstract cooperators" who speak of hope and what the possibilities are who try to act in good conscience and reach goals without compromising their ethics. "William McKinley, in contrast, is a fine example of the steadfast Guardian temperament, and joins the distinguished company of American Presidents like George Washington, Grover Cleveland, and Harry Truman, all sober and serious men."[69]

Idealists:

Considered "abstract cooperators" who think and act in terms of hope and possibilities. They try to act ethically and reach their

---

[67] Ibid Kerisy and Choiniere.
[68] http://www.keirsey.com/4temps/overview_temperaments.asp
[69] Ibid. Keirsey

objectives honestly. Keirsey and Choiniere were unable to find any Presidents they considered to be "idealists." The closest leaders as examples would be Eleanor Roosevelt and Mahatma Gandhi.

Artisans:
Are "concrete utilitarians" who deal in what they can see and touch and will act according to whatever will work, in particular, what results in an immediate payoff, even if rules have to be twisted. Presidents in this category are daring, colorful and charming with charisma like Teddy Roosevelt, Andrew Jackson, John F. Kennedy, Lyndon Johnson, and Ronald Reagan.

Rational:
They are "abstract utilitarians" who speak about new challenges and new solutions. They are pragmatic and efficient and will ignore conventions and rules if necessary to get the job done "Rational, has given us some of our most far-sighted and controversial Presidents, men of theory and strategy such as Thomas Jefferson, James Madison, and Abraham Lincoln."[70]

According to Kerisey and Choiniere, Presidents are born with a certain temperament which has more bearing on their behavior than their background, education, social status and economic conditions and the general conditions of their times. Most biographers dwell on achievements and the era in which a President lives. Instead, temperament is a major factor in how they act and what they do. "Something is missed when the qualities of the seed and the tree, of temperament and character, are overlooked."[71]

---

[70] Ibid. Keirsey
[71] Ibid. Keirsey

President Dwight David Eisenhower, Courtesy Library of Congress

The most important point is that it is character that separates leaders who even have similar backgrounds. Truman, Eisenhower and Lyndon Johnson came from rural upbringings and struggled in families that could barely make ends meet.

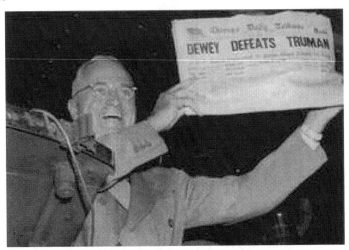

President Harry Truman after winning the 1948 election, Courtesy Library of Congress

Their temperaments governed their time in the White House: Johnson had an Artisan temperament, Truman a Guardian character and Eisenhower exhibited a Rational nature. Those who came from a patrician background demonstrated similar differences: John Kennedy (Artisan), Carter (Guardian) and Thomas Jefferson (Rational). Johnson, for instance, was often cunning and quite different from Eisenhower who was self-controlled. JFK was stylish while Carter was moralistic. Each could relate to one another in terms of disposition: JFK could understand LBJ and could take each other's measure. Eisenhower could appreciate an aristocratic Jefferson who was a designer of buildings who could create the University of Virginia.

Character, as a result, involves a lifelong pattern of behavior. As we have seen, once we determine the temperament of a President we can forecast, to a large extent, their behavior. Their actions are spontaneous parts of their predisposition to perform in a certain way. "Thus the innately vigorous Artisan Teddy Roosevelt could rejoice, 'A President has a great chance; his position is that of a king and a prime minister rolled into one,' and his habitual behavior would consistently reflect this dynamic Artisan perspective."[72]

President Calvin Coolidge, Courtesy Library of Congress

Calvin Coolidge: Example of A Guardian President

Calvin Coolidge was a perfect example of the Guardian temperament. He entered the White House in 1921 and left it as President. President Warren G. Harding died in San Francisco in august, 1923 while Vice President Coolidge was with his father and family in the family farmhouse in Vermont. Coolidge showed his

---

[72] Ibid. Keirsey

qualities as a person and leader when he recalled that momentous night in his memoirs:

"On the night of August 2, 1923, I was awakened by my father coming up the stairs, calling my name. I noticed that his voice trembled. As the only times I had ever observed that before were when death had visited our family, I knew that something of the gravest nature had occurred. He placed in my hands an official report and told me that President Harding had just passed away. My wife and I at once dressed.

Before leaving the room I knelt down and, with the same prayer with which I have since approached the altar of the church, asked God to bless the American people and give me power to serve them.

My first thought was to express my sympathy for those who had been bereaved and after that was done to attempt to reassure the country with the knowledge that I proposed no sweeping displacement of the men then in office and that there were to be no violent changes in the administration of affairs. As soon as I had dispatched a telegram to Mrs. Harding, I therefore issued a short public statement declaratory of that purpose.

Coolidge was a cautious and pessimistic President who protected his territory, the United States of America. He was concerned with its welfare and future. It was natural for him to warn the nation in 1928 that even though it was enjoying prosperity, all could be easily lost.

Calvin Coolidge being sworn in as President of the United States by a Notary Public on August 2, 1923 on the death of President Warren G. Harding, Courtesy the Library of Congress

A year later it was in the Wall Street Crash of 1929. By then, Herbert Hoover was in office.

In the same manner, it was natural for Thomas Jefferson to be a visionary and long range planner. "So Jefferson could declare that the United States was not merely another nation, but an 'experiment to show whether man can be trusted with self-government.'" [73]

---

[73] Ibid. Keirsey

Maine Senator Edmond Muskie, Courtesy of the US Senate

The Fall of Edmond Muskie

One of the leading candidates for the nomination of the Democratic Party in the 1972 Presidential campaign was Maine Senator Edmond Muskie. He was considered a man of character and integrity. He was a victim of a "dirty trick" committed by Kenneth W. Clawson, a political aid of President Richard Nixon. Muskie was viewed as a strong challenger to Nixon's chances of reelection.

Courtesy of Pat Oliphant and the Susan Conway Gallery of Washington, D.C.

Throughout the New Hampshire campaign, the Manchester Union Leader attacked him. In an anonymous letter he was accused of using the pejorative term "Canuck" in referring to the state's French Canadians. It was later discovered that Clawson had sent the letter to discredit Muskie. The paper also published an article accusing Muskie's wife of "unladylike" behavior. Muskie cracked.

A week before the New Hampshire primary, he hired a flatbed truck and stood before the Union Leader building in the snow. He passionately defended his wife and criticized the publisher and his paper. He then began to weep, according to some reporters. Muskie won the primary but his poll numbers began to fall. He left the race six weeks after the campaign had begun.

The Senator's temperament was challenged. It was clear that he was a man of integrity but doubts rose about his ability to control himself under pressure. He later said he had choked up over his anger. "It changed people's minds about me," he said about the incident. "They were looking for a strong, steady man, and here I was weak." [74]

Vice President Spiro Agnew, Courtesy Office of the Vice President

The Resignation of Spiro Agnew

In the case of Spiro Agnew, Vice President under Richard Nixon, his character was challenged by an incident that happened as Governor of Maryland. He was accused of taking bribes in the form of campaign contributions from companies that won state contracts.

---

[74] https://www.washingtonpost.com/wp-srv/politics/special/clinton/frenzy/muskie.htm

Spiro Agnew Political Cartoon Courtesy DeSoto, 1973

By 1973, President Nixon was facing impeachment for the Watergate cover up. The prospect of a simultaneous impeachment of the Vice President and President was real. Agnew pleaded "nolo contendere" to the charges against him, which meant that he acknowledged his guilt. He paid a $160,000 for back taxes and a $10,000 fine and was spared going to jail.

On October 10th, 1973, he became the second Vice President to resign from office. John C. Calhoun left to take a Senate seat. Agnew quit in the face of criminal charges of tax evasion and bribery of a public official.[75] Later he was disbarred from the State of Maryland, calling him "morally obtuse."[76]

President Gerald Ford, Courtesy Library of Congress

---

[75] Agnew, Spiro T., *Go Quietly....or else*, William Morrow, New York, 1980 p. 15.
[76] ABA Journal May 2009, http://www.abajournal.com/magazine/article/may_2_1974/

Gerald Ford: Vice President

Agnew was succeeded by Gerald Ford, Republican House Minority leader and a man with a reputation of honesty and character. James Cannon described the selection this way: [77]

Gerald R. Ford became President not because he was popular with the American public, not because he campaigned for the job, but because of his character.

More than any other president of this century, Ford was chosen for his integrity and trustworthiness; his peers in Congress put him in the White House because he told the truth and kept his word… Ford personified what Nixon was not. Ford was honest. He could be trusted. Throughout twenty-five years in the House of Representatives, Ford had proved himself to be a man of integrity. It was for that integrity that the highest powers of Congress, Democratic and Republican, chose Ford to be Vice President, knowing that Nixon's presidency was doomed……

President Richard Nixon announces the release of the Watergate Tapes, April 29th, 1974, Courtesy National Archives

[77] Cannon, James, Character Above All,
http://www.pbs.org/newshour/spc/character/essays/ford.html

Richard Nixon: Watergate

The Watergate scandal was one of the biggest in US history involving a President. Five men were caught breaking into Democrat National Party Headquarters in 1972. A subsequent investigation discovered that Richard Nixon attempted to cover up information about the affair.   The scandal grew costing Nixon much of his political support. He resigned on August 9th, 1974 in the face of possible impeachment and removal from office. The incident revealed much about Nixon's character. Nixon appeared cunning, secretive and paranoiac. He was accused of using the Office of the President to punish political enemies and gain political gain. He was forced to deliver tapes that recorded conversations he had in the White House that ultimately showed his involvement in the Watergate break-in.

Gene Basset, 1974 Courtesy United Features Syndicate

James MacGregor Burns observed of Nixon, "How can one evaluate such an idiosyncratic president, so brilliant and so morally lacking?" [78] Nixon's biographers disagree on how he will be perceived by history. According to Ambrose, "Nixon wanted to be judged by what he accomplished. What he will be remembered for is the nightmare he put the country through in his second term and for his resignation."[79] Historian Keith W. Olson has written that Nixon left a negative legacy: fundamental mistrust of government with its roots in Vietnam and Watergate.[80]

George Washington summed it up:

"In times of turbulence, when the passions are afloat, calm reason is swallowed up in the extremes to which measures are attempted to be carried; but when those subside and the empire of it is resumed, the man who acts from principle, who pursues the paths of truth, moderation, and justice, will regain his influence."[81]

---

[78] Skidmore, Max J. (2001). "Ranking and Evaluating Presidents: The Case of Theodore Roosevelt". *White House Studies* 1 (4), p.495

[79] Ambrose, Stephen E. (1991). *Nixon: Ruin and Recovery 1973–1990*. New York: Simon & Schuster. ISBN 978-0-671-69188-2, p.492

[80] Parmet, Herbert S. (1990). *Richard Nixon and His America*. Boston: Little, Brown & Co. ISBN 978-0-316-69232-8, p. 81

[81] From a letter from Washington to John Jay, May 18, 1786. Quoted in *The Life of John Marshall*, Albert J. Beveridge, Houghton Mifflin, Boston, 1919, vol. I, p. 307. http://www.leaderu.com/humanities/foundersview.html

President William Jefferson Clinton, State of the Union Address, 1997, Courtesy Library of Congress

Character is a journey, not a destination. **William J. Clinton**

The Impeachment of Bill Clinton

Bill Clinton was one of the most popular Presidents in US history. He had a strong record of achievement and was judged on his accomplishments.

Tom Toles 1994 cartoon, Clinton was all things to all people, Courtesy Conservapedia

He was elected twice and managed to maintain a sound economy and a distinctive foreign policy. Even so, he was plagued by questions about his character before and during his time in the White House. Several women came forward during the campaign accusing him of affairs. There were allegations of misuse of campaign funds and improprieties when he was Governor of Arkansas.

In the White House, he demonstrated that he was by far the most one of the most successful political fund raisers in Presidential history. Another scandal developed from this when he was accused of making the Lincoln Bedroom available for overnight stays to contributors. The Democratic Party was also forced to return donations from foreign sources raised by Clinton.

Readings of the articles of impeachment against President Clinton in the Senate, January, 1999. This was the second time in US history a President faced impeachment, Courtesy National Archives.

His gravest challenge was when he faced impeachment based on allegations of perjury and obstruction of justice arising from his affair with intern Monica Lewinsky. Clinton was exonerated.[82]On his last day in office, January 20th, 2001, President Clinton issued 141 pardon and 36 commutations, some of which were highly questionable.[83]

Bill Neikirk of the Chicago Tribune commented on Clinton's legacy:[84]

Admired by friend and foe for his political skills, Clinton survived eight bruising years of scandal and partisan clashes with congressional Republicans while presiding over one of the best economies in U.S. history...Clinton brought to Washington a new style of governing, the so-called permanent campaign, in which partisan charge is met with partisan countercharge and legislative battles are often fought like political races. Sometimes this worked to win passage of legislation, but sometimes it created hard feelings and a lack of compromise.

---

[82] Clinton's Legacy after 8 Years in Office: Peace, Prosperity and Impeachment, December 14, 2000|By William Neikirk, Washington Bureau. http://articles.chicagotribune.com/2000-12-14/news/0012140240_1_clinton-and-gore-legacy-bill-clinton/2

[83] "Clinton pardons: Cast of characters". BBC News Online. February 22, 2001. September 11, 2011.

[84] ibid Neikirk

"It's a destructive cycle that has been unleashed in American politics," said Rep. Mark Sanford (R-S.C.), and it appears to be here to stay in a world of 24-hour news cycles, he said... Bill Clinton's legacy as president has been burnished by peace and prosperity, tarnished by impeachment, and ... diminished by the failure of Vice President Al Gore to succeed him.

The Nixon and Clinton examples are clear. Character, which includes truthfulness, integrity, a strong sense of ethical behavior, is absolutely essential for a President of the United States. Past words and actions often predict what their administration will look like and what measures they will take. The "blackmail factor" is also a serious concern. A President who plays loose with the truth and morals subjects himself and the nation to extortion.

This is a risk that should never be taken.

In "The Double-Edged Sword, How Character Makes and Ruins Presidents, From Washington to Clinton," Robert Shogan explained the importance of character:[85]

Yet for all the distortions and confusions surrounding the character issue during the Clinton presidency, the constant controversy serves only to underline the reality that presidential character remains a powerful element in the political system and, given the limitations of that system, a potentially constructive force. Moreover, given the highly personalized nature of the U.S. political system, politicians and scholars alike argue that there is no better way of choosing a candidate for president than by evaluating what kind of human being he--or she--really is. "Voters know that the issues a president will have to face will change in time," Robert Teeter, a GOP pollster and senior Bush campaign strategist, once told me. "But his character will always be there." And these words from a contemporary political operative reflect thinking that has prevailed in the Republic since its founders met two centuries ago in Constitution Hall.

The qualities of a great man are vision, integrity, courage, understanding, the power of articulation, and profundity of character.   **Dwight Eisenhower**

Character is a word that seems to define almost all human activity and then some...Power is what you do and character is what you

---

[85] The Double-Edged Sword, How Character Makes and Ruins Presidents, From Washington to Clinton By Robert Shogan, Westview Press, New York, Chapter One, https://www.nytimes.com/books/first/s/shogan-sword.html

are... All leaders must face some crisis where their own strength of character is the enemy.   **Richard Reeves**

...what's in a person's heart and soul will not likely be changed by the ability to command a helicopter to land on the South Lawn."

Robert Dallek

The (ancient) Greeks believed that character was formed in part by fate and in part by parental training, and that character was exemplified not only by acts of bravery in battle but in the habits of daily conduct.   **James Cannon**

In a president, character is everything. A president doesn't have to be brilliant... He doesn't have to be clever; you can hire clever... You can hire pragmatic, and you can buy and bring in policy wonks. But you can't buy courage and decency; you can't rent a strong moral sense. A president must bring those things with him... He needs to have, in that much maligned word, but a good one nonetheless, a "vision" of the future he wishes to create... But a vision is worth little if a president doesn't have the character-- the courage and heart-- to see it through.   **Peggy Noonan**

The challenge for us in 2016 is discovering the character of the candidates to see if their temperaments are what we need today. Do we need a "guardian" who will seek cooperation and will follow rules carefully? Is an "idealist" who preaches hope and optimism to reach our goals what we require? Would a pragmatic, charismatic "artisan" who looks for immediate results in spite of the obstacles be more appropriate for our time of rapid change? Or would we be better off with a

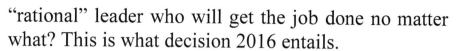
"rational" leader who will get the job done no matter what? This is what decision 2016 entails.

Chapter Six: Visionary

Vision is the art of seeing what is invisible to others. J. Swift

Leadership is the capacity to translate vision into reality.

Warren Bennis

You are not here merely to make a living. You are here in order to enable the world to live more amply, with greater vision, with a finer spirit of hope and achievement. You are here to enrich the world, and you impoverish yourself if you forget the errand.

Woodrow Wilson

Failed plans should not be interpreted as a failed vision. Visions don't change, they are only refined. Plans rarely stay the same, and are scrapped or adjusted as needed. Be stubborn about the vision, but flexible with your plan.   **John C. Maxwell**

Where there is no vision, there is no hope. **George W. Carver**

If art is to nourish the roots of our culture, society must set the artist free to follow his vision wherever it takes him.

John F. Kennedy

Vision without action is a daydream. Action without vision is a nightmare. **Japanese Proverb**

The only thing worse than being blind is having sight but no vision.
Helen Keller

Our most effective Presidents have had a compelling vision that they transmitted to the nation to harness the energy and support of the people and the country's political institutions to reach new goals. A President must have the wherewithal to carry out his or her vision. They need a team of experts to help them govern and garner congressional support for their policies. They must focus on a few key issues and get them approved and implemented. Bill Clinton, for instance, stated from the start of his administration that one of his objectives was to balance the budget and develop a close relationship with business while still maintaining social programs. Others Presidents projected the same sort of aspirations. An example is the US space program.

Apollo XI moon landing, July 20th, 1969, Courtesy National Archives

Things do not happen. Things are made to happen.

John F. Kennedy

John F. Kennedy: A Man on the Moon

On May 25th, 1961, President John F. Kennedy delivered a special message before Congress. He asked for additional funds to begin a concerted effort to create a new space program. He said:[86]

I believe that this nation should commit itself to achieving the goal, before this decade is out, of landing a man on the moon and returning him safely to the earth. No single space project in this period will be more impressive to mankind, or more important for the long-range exploration of space.

John F. Kennedy

---

[86] John F. Kennedy's Vision of Peace, On the 50th anniversary of JFK's death, his nephew recalls the fallen president's attempts to halt the war machine, By Robert F. Kennedy Jr. November 20, 2013, http://www.rollingstone.com/politics/news/john-f-kennedys-vision-of-peace-20131120

There were some who questioned the National Aeronautics and Space Administration's (NASA) ability to achieve this vision. Yet, within 12 months, Gus Grissom and Alan Shepard became the first two US astronauts to travel into space. In February, 1962, John Glenn orbited the earth. He circled the planet three times in four hours and piloted his spaceship, Friendship 7, back into earth's atmosphere landing in the Atlantic. His success inspired more attempts to successfully venture into space.

President John Fitzgerald Kennedy, Courtesy JFK Library

Eight years after Kennedy launched his vision for a lunar landing, Apollo 11 astronauts, Armstrong, Collins and Aldrin landed on moon on July 20th, 1969, realizing JFK's dream.

A man may die, nations may rise and fall, but an idea lives on.

John F. Kennedy

President Ronald Reagan, Courtesy Ronald Reagan Presidential Library

I call upon the scientific community in our country, those who gave us nuclear weapons, to turn their great talents now to the cause of mankind and world peace: to give us the means of rendering these nuclear weapons impotent and obsolete.

Ronald Reagan

Ronald Reagan's Vision for America

Ronald Reagan had a vision for America. He expressed it on November 3rd, 1980. It was the night before the election. [87] He began his address by speaking to the people about his faith in our nation's values and our sense of patriotism and our achievements. He knew that some had doubts about the America's future. He wanted to sweep away any concerns. Reagan asked a question and

---

[87] Ronald Reagan: "Election Eve Address "A Vision for America"," November 3, 1980. Online by Gerhard Peters and John T. Woolley, *The American Presidency Project.* http://www.presidency.ucsb.edu/ws/?pid=85199

then provided the answer: "the question before us tonight... does history still has a place for America, for her people, for her great ideals?"[88]

Ronald Reagan laid out the principles of freedom and democracy and justice that he felt were at the heart of the American dream. He explained how the dream was still there and would be realized by a government that reduced excessive spending, diminished taxes, fortified its military, worked closely with the Congress and sought peace with all nations through strength and understanding. Reagan ended his address to the voters by stressing our common beliefs in our nation's future. He saw America as the "last best hope of man on earth."

He spoke of those Americans visiting Washington and looking at those symbols of greatness from the White House to the Congress to the Lincoln Memorial as they repeated his words, "Let us bind up the nation's wounds." He ended his speech this way: [89]

At this very moment, some young American, coming up along the Virginia or Maryland shores of the Potomac is seeing for the first time the lights that glow on the great halls of our government and the monuments to the memory of our great men.

Let us resolve tonight that young Americans will always see those Potomac lights; that they will always find there a city of hope in a country that is free. And let us resolve they will say of our day and our generation that we did keep faith with our God, that we did act "worthy of ourselves;" that we did protect and pass on lovingly that shining city on a hill.

Reagan won the election with 489 electoral votes against 49 for Carter, carrying 44 states and receiving over 50% of the popular vote against Carter's 41%. Reagan's party captured the Senate and gained seats in the House where the Democrats retained control.

---

[88] Ibid. Peters and Woolley
[89] Ibid. Peters and Woolley

IT'S MOURNING in AMERICA
Ronald Reagan
1911~2004

Cartoon by Steve Benson 2004, Courtesy Political Memes

Reagan labored to fulfill his promises. He worked with an opposition Congress to pass legislation to lower taxes and stimulate economic growth, curb inflation, deregulate economic activity, shrink government spending while expanding military expenditures. During his eight years in office, inflation fell from 12.5% to 3.4% and average annual real GDP growth was over 3.4%. [90] He won re-election with the largest Electoral College victory in history. When he left office in 1989, Ronald Reagan departed with an approval rating of 68% comparable to that of FDR and Bill Clinton.

Freedom is never more than one generation away from extinction. We didn't pass it to our children in the bloodstream. It must be fought for, protected, and handed on for them to do the same.

Ronald Reagan

---

[90] Murray, Robert K.; Tim H. Blessing (1993). Greatness in the White House. Penn State Press, p. 80.

President Theodore Roosevelt, Courtesy the White House

Great thoughts speak only to the thoughtful mind, but great actions speak to all mankind.... Believe you can and you're halfway there.

Far better is it to dare mighty things, to win glorious triumphs, even though checkered by failure... than to rank with those poor spirits who neither enjoy nor suffer much, because they live in a gray twilight that knows not victory nor defeat.

We must treat each man on his worth and merits as a man. We must see that each is given a **square deal***, because he is entitled to no more and should receive no less.* **Theodore Roosevelt**

Theodore Roosevelt and the Square Deal

The 26th President of the United States came into office after the assassination of William McKinley. He was the youngest man to ever occupy the Office. At first, he pledged to continue his predecessor's policies. Soon he discovered that he had a different vision for America. Theodore Roosevelt was a man of energy and adventure. He was audacious and exuberant and saw the nation he governed through the same eyes. Roosevelt possessed amazing mental and physical vigor. He was a man of action. He did not hesitate to make a decision, plot a course and follow it until it was concluded. The Presidency for Theodore Roosevelt was a "Bully Pulpit."

From that vantage point he could shape and direct the course of the nation with his ideas, his ideals and his immense capacity to move forward in all directions simultaneously. He was at the same time, a writer, a student, a negotiator, a doer and a thinker. He believed that the President should set the example in all things and guide the republic to new heights of opportunity and social justice.

Roosevelt cast his vision for America in his "Square Deal." As the century turned from the 19th to the 20th he could see the direction of the United States as the juggernaut of the industrial revolution raced forward engulfing workers, the environment, resources and institutions. He saw his mission as controlling savage capitalism, protecting the rights of workers, safeguarding the health and welfare of all Americans and securing the rights granted in the Constitution to the weak and downtrodden. The spirit of the Square

Deal was about the future. It was about opening up new possibilities and not being afraid of the unknown.

A CROWN HE IS ENTITLED TO WEAR.

According to the "Almanac of Theodore Roosevelt," he was the first President to own an automobile and ride in an airplane. He dove in a submarine; installed a phone in his home; and was the first to travel outside the US while in office and the first President to receive the first electoral vote cast by a woman delegate. He advocated a Jewish homeland in Palestine; fought for the creation of the League of Nations and was the first US President to play host to the Olympics. He broke ground on the largest public works project in history, the Panama Canal. He wrote thirty books and a 150,000 letters.

Theodore Roosevelt was the first American citizen to win the Nobel Price and the first and only President to win the Congressional Medal of Honor. The highest award given by the NCAA bears the name of Theodore Roosevelt. He is featured on the bonds of the United States. His picture is on the $1 Million US Treasury Bill and T Bond.[91]

Roosevelt won the election of 1904 by a landslide and continued his vision for America by securing the place of the US in the world as a great power. He launched the "Great White Fleet," negotiated the peace treaty ending the Russo Japanese war and led a foreign policy of peace with respect and strength. He left the White House in 1908 as one of the most popular leaders in American history.

Mount Rushmore: Washington, Jefferson, Theodore Roosevelt and Lincoln, Courtesy the Library of Congress

Theodore Roosevelt was an American nationalist who projected a view of America as an exceptional country that could succeed in all it ventured. His strategy focused on the President as a visionary and

---

[91] http://www.theodore-roosevelt.com/trbioqf.html, The Almanac of Theodore Roosevelt website.

active participant in the life of the nation. His legacy of courage and tenacity of the American spirit has carried on to the present day.

Vision and strategy are both important. But there is a priority to them. Vision always comes first. Always. If you have a clear vision, you will eventually attract the right strategy. If you don't have a clear vision, no strategy will save you. **Michael Hyatt**

2016 should be the year when a new President projected a vision for America for the rest of this century. The domestic and foreign policy trials that America will encounter demand direction. Our new Commander in Chief must visualize and express where we must go and how we will get there in foreign and domestic affairs, social and economic policy and the preservation of freedom and democracy that our republic and people need to be assured about.

Chapter Seven: Emotional Intelligence

If your emotional abilities aren't in hand, if you don't have self-awareness, if you are not able to manage your distressing emotions, if you can't have empathy and have effective relationships, then no matter how smart you are, you are not going to get very far.
Daniel Goleman

What makes a leader? ...self-awareness, which both lets you know your strengths and limits, and strengthens your inner ethical radar; self-management, which lets you lead yourself effectively; and empathy, which lets you read other people accurately. You put all those together in every act of leadership. **Daniel Goleman**

As human beings we all want to be happy and free from misery... we have learned that the key to happiness is inner peace. The greatest obstacles to inner peace are disturbing emotions such as anger, attachment, fear and suspicion, while love and compassion and a sense of universal responsibility are the sources of peace and happiness. **Dalai Lama**

Sooner or later, those who win are those who think they can.
Richard Bach

Harmonious Emotional Engagement is the tool that allows leaders to take full advantage of these three simple but profound principles: People respond emotionally to every situation that occurs in an organization. People's negative emotions reduce their performance in an organization. People's positive emotions enhance their performance in an organization. **Timothy Warneka**

We often hear that men are unfit to govern themselves. Are they then fit to govern others? **Thomas Jefferson**

The Components of Emotional Intelligence

A President who wishes to lead others must first be able to lead themselves. Knowing and managing ourselves is the key. Emotional intelligence is at the epitome of Presidential Leadership. It allows us to tap into our emotions and those of others. Daniel Goleman defined emotional intelligence as consisting of five components: [92]

Self-Awareness:
Understanding and recognizing personal emotions, moods and drives and their impact on others. This includes honest self-assessment, a self-deprecating sense of humor and self-confidence.

Self-Regulation:
Suspending judgement and thinking before acting and the ability to redirect and control moods, feelings and impulses. Characteristics include integrity, comfort with ambiguity and change and trustworthiness.

Internal Motivation:
An inner drive that does not involve external rewards. It consists of a passion for work that does not involve status and money but entails an inner vision of life's priorities like the love of learning; curiosity; the joy of achievement and activity; pursuit of goals and persistence and energy. Traits are optimism, a powerful drive to accomplish, even in the face of failure, and loyalty to an institution and its objectives.

---

[92] Salon, on June 28, 1999, Daniel Goleman, the Five Components of Emotional Intelligence, http://www.sonoma.edu/users/s/swijtink/teaching/philosophy_101/paper1/goleman.htm

2016 Selecting the President

Empathy:

Comprehending the emotional temperament of others and treating people based on their emotional responses. Qualities are retaining talent, cross-cultural understanding, sincere sympathy, service to others and altruism.

Social Skills:

Ability to build and manage relationships, find common ground for understanding and creating support. Traits are success in handling change, the ability to persuade and the skill in constructing and leading teams.

When it comes to having emotional intelligence we must match it with normal, rational behavior and overall health. The White House is no place for those who are emotionally disturbed or have severe mental illnesses or are not physically fit to handle the enormous responsibilities of President of the United States. Those who have emotional intelligence also have the wisdom to know how to maintain equilibrium by relaxing and resting sufficiently. Lincoln went to the theater, John Kennedy and Franklin Roosevelt loved sailing. In each case, they focused on relieving the great burden of responsibility to preserve their mental and physical strength to carry out their duties.

Several Presidents exhibited the form of strong *emotional intelligence* explained by Goleman. They include Lincoln, Jefferson, Washington, Kennedy, Franklin Roosevelt and Theodore Roosevelt.[93]

---

[93] Bruce R. Posten, The power of EQ: Emotional intelligence can make big difference in president's success http://www2.readingeagle.com/article.aspx?id=125717

Abraham Lincoln, Courtesy Library of Congress

Nearly all men can stand adversity, but if you want to test a man's character give him power. **Abraham Lincoln**

Lincoln's Strength, Empathy, Compassion and Moral Compass

Lincoln had high morals, kindness, steadfastness, vision, sterling character and wisdom. His leadership was challenged constantly. He certainly had powerful emotional intelligence to deal with the endless obstacles and difficulties that would have overcome most leaders. For example, he suffered from: the loss of his young sons; the division of the Union; defeats on the battlefield; the enormous causalities of the war; the criticism of the press, his staff and his cabinet and the capricious behavior of his wife.

Abraham's dream!–"Coming events cast their shadows before" 1864, Currier and Ives

He handled constant setbacks by staying focused on his goals: win the war, preserve the union, end slavery and reconstruction. He set aside egos, ambitions and conflicts in his Cabinet and personal attacks on him by staying the course on his vision which he constantly articulated and explained. Lincoln rarely insisted that he was right when others contested his opinions and decisions. He listened and was ready to change his mind if need be.

Often times, Lincoln would write a letter channeling his emotions and venting his anger when he was opposed or criticized. He would save it for a day or two and rarely send it. It gave him time to cool down and use reason and common sense and not make rash judgements that would result in more conflict.

One of his greatest talents was his ability to listen patiently to both sides of an argument. Those who had the opportunity to discuss issues with him felt that Lincoln gave them the chance to express themselves even if he disagreed. He spoke in simple, clear language that his audience could understand and learn from. He never spoke above his audience. He used stories and metaphors to transform complex ideas into simple concepts that all could grasp.

Lincoln was a skillful mediator. He brought those of differing opinions together to discuss and resolve issues. He showed a remarkable ability to consider the feelings of others. He made it a point to mend fences with his enemies and not humiliate them in the process. He had the courage to be kind.

Perhaps his greatest emotional strength was his humility. He was self-confident enough to admit and learn from his errors and flexible enough to change course. He always took responsibility. He admitted his mistakes and did not dwell on them or those of others. He preferred to move on and get the job done.

As the Civil War drew to a conclusion, Abraham Lincoln did not gloat over his victory. He went to great lengths to avoid humiliating the South and its leaders. General Robert E. Lee, for example, was treated with dignity. Confederate soldiers were allowed to go home with their possessions.

On February 15, 1865, the New York Times wrote about Lincoln and his emotional intelligence and his place in history:[94]

In fact, when we take into account the circumstances in which Mr. LINCOLN has been placed, the provocations he has received, the excitement in the midst of which he has lived, and the vile and blackguard personal abuse which has during the last four years been showered on him, both here and in Europe, it will always reflect the highest honor on him, as well as on the people whom he represents, that he has never once been betrayed into violent or even impatient language. We believe his speeches and letters may be searched in vain for the smallest indication of passion or vexation. There are many things in them which a scholar or man of high culture would, perhaps, have omitted, or have uttered differently; but nothing which a gentleman might regret or feel ashamed of. This consolation, and it is a great one, he will at least carry with him into his retirement…

---

[94] The New York Times, February 15th, 1865, Jefferson Davis and Lincoln, http://www.nytimes.com/1865/02/15/news/jefferson-davis-abraham-lincoln.html

Thomas Jefferson, Courtesy Library of Congress

Nothing can stop the man with the right mental attitude from achieving his goal; nothing on earth can help the man with the wrong mental attitude.

Do you want to know who you are? Don't ask. Act! Action will delineate and define you.

Honesty is the first chapter in the book of wisdom. **Jefferson**

Thomas Jefferson: A Model of Presidential Leadership

"When a group of Nobel laureates visited the White House during his administration, John F. Kennedy remarked, 'I think this is the most extraordinary collection of talent, of human knowledge, that has ever been gathered together at the White House, with the possible exception of when Thomas Jefferson dined alone.'"[95]

Jefferson was a founding father, principle author of the Declaration of the Independence. He reflected strong emotional intelligence throughout his life and certainly during his Presidency. He was multitalented and multifaceted. In each of Jefferson's activities he had to exhibit self-control and self-restraint. He was a model of Presidential leadership.

Abraham Lincoln articulated Jefferson's principles of liberty and freedom as the reasons to preserve the Union. He called him, "the most distinguished politician in our history." [96] He was a Renaissance man who was skilled in so many areas, in addition to politics. One of Jefferson's biographers called him a man who "could calculate an eclipse, survey an estate, tie an artery, plan an edifice, try a cause, break a horse, dance a minuet, and play the violin."[97]

Professor James Barber wrote about Jefferson's achievements as President and cited him as one of the most accomplished leaders in our history because he "was able to apply his reason to organizing connections with Congress and was thus able to express a clear and open vision of what the country could be with a profound political

---

[95]John F. Kennedy, Remarks at a Dinner Honoring Nobel Prize Winners of the Western Hemisphere, April 29th, 1962.
http://www.presidency.ucsb.edu/ws/?pid=8623

[96] Ibid. John F. Kennedy,
[97] Ibid. John F. Kennedy,

sense."[98] Jefferson was able to interact with all types of people at all levels. He dealt with policy advocates in Congress, with politicians and ordinary people. He had a clear sense of vision and was able to portray it with common sense and pragmatism.

"In a paper on Presidential leadership, Sarah Ofosu-Ameyaw, describes how, 'Jefferson's ability to apply reason and clearly express his vision of what this country should be, shows that he is indeed an individual who had a high level of emotional intelligence; he was emotionally self-aware, assertive, he had a high self-regard, he was capable of problem solving, and he had good impulse control.'"[99] This was the key to his success. He was able to empathize and sympathize, manage his emotions and comprehend those of others.

Few American presidents are held in higher esteem than Thomas Jefferson... he holds an unshakable place in the pantheon of American heroes.   **Robert Dallek**

Jefferson had almost single-handedly provided "a mine of legislative wealth" that provided Virginians with a modern republic built on the foundations of Greece and Rome... Jefferson, in short, in his legal laboratory atop Monticello, invented the United States of America."   **Willard Sterne Randall**

Other Presidents also exhibited the kind of emotional intelligence that helped guide America during its most difficult times.

---

[98] Russel Razzague, MD, Top 3 Emotionally Intelligent Presidents In US History Part 1: Thomas Jefferson https://www.psychologytoday.com/blog/political-intelligence/201203/top-3-emotionally-intelligent-presidents-in-us-history-part-1

[99] Ibid Razzague.

George Washington, Courtesy Library of Congress

The Self Confidence of George Washington

His strength of character commanded the kind of respect and awe necessary for our first President. Washington proved on the battlefield and in the field of politics that he had self-control, self-respect and respect and admiration for others. His self-confidence allowed him to deal with the strong personalities of his Cabinet and face the challenges of the young republic he led. He understood the use of power and set the foundation for the Presidency to be occupied by those who were patriotic, experienced, honorable and committed to sacrificing all they had for the United States.

Franklin Delano Roosevelt, Courtesy Library of Congress

The Resilience of FDR

Justice Oliver Wendell Holmes said: "FDR had a second-class intellect but a first class temperament." [100]   His charm, wit, charisma, ability to communicate and his skill at self-control gave him the strength to deal with the tremendous challenges of the Great Depression and World War II. Our nation was fortunate that he was at the helm during those critical times and surrounded himself with advisers who have emotional intelligence to tackle the critical problems of his era.

---

[100] Ibid Posten

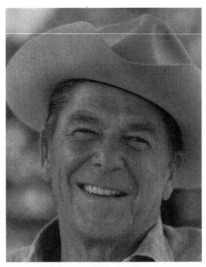

Ronald Reagan, Courtesy Reagan Presidential Library

The Optimism of Ronald Reagan

He projected a simple, friendly, optimistic personality. He conveyed trustworthiness and rarely took himself seriously. Like Lincoln, he used humor to make a point and drive home an idea. Mikhail Gorbachev described Reagan this way: "While adhering to his convictions, Reagan was not dogmatic; he was looking for negotiation and compromise." Those who worked with him found him kind, humble and a decent person who was devoid of pettiness and meanness. He admitted mistakes and moved on. Ronald Reagan sought a balanced and full life while leading the nation. He had the emotional intelligence to do both. [101]

Dr. Heather Uczynski has studied the emotional intelligence of a number of Presidents. Her observations are interesting in that they

---

[101] Ibid Posten

clearly demonstrate that without it a President cannot handle the awesome burden of responsibilities that go with the job.[102]

Dwight David Eisenhower, Courtesy Library of Congress

IKE's Ability to Persuade without Dominating

According to Uczynski, Eisenhower had the ability to be persuasive without being domineering. He had a way of saying the right things to elicit cooperation and trust. As Supreme Allied Commander in World War II he had to contend with numerous personalities and political leaders to harness the energy of the allies to win the War. He was a natural leader with a strong character matched by a good nature. His experience as a military leader and administrator gave him the skills to organize the White House and set up a team to deal with the growing challenges of the Cold War.

---

[102] Ibid Posten

Theodore Roosevelt, Courtesy Library of Congress

Theodore Roosevelt: Powerful Emotional Intelligence

Uczynski judged Teddy Roosevelt as one "perfectly fitted for his times." He had powerful emotional intelligence which he exhibited by his energy, decisiveness and assertiveness. He was self-aware but seemed, at times, lack self-control.[103] Teddy was a volcano of energy. He maintained a vigorous schedule of meetings, speeches, physical and mental activity and constantly making decisions. He exhibited fearlessness and a profound vision of where America should be going and how to get there. Roosevelt consistently articulated his vision of a strong, free and prosperous country that was creative and compassionate. He matched his rhetoric with actions like flying in the first plane to promote the new technology and passing legislation to build the Panama Canal to unite the East and West Coasts into a well-organized system of trade on the high seas that would expand global commerce and make America more secure militarily and economically.

---

[103] Ibid Posten

Courtesy Truman Library

Truman: Unafraid to Decide

Harry Truman had very strong emotional intelligence and was not afraid to make decisions and move forward, even if they were not of political benefit to him or his Party. He was disciplined, and had very high integrity and self-confidence and respect for the Office of President. After the death of Franklin Roosevelt, Harry Truman was left with the tasks to end the Wars in Europe and Japan and secure a post-war peace. He did so by making tough but well thought out decisions. They required the discipline and rigor to choose alternatives based on facts and stick to them. This demanded steadfastness on his part and those of his team.

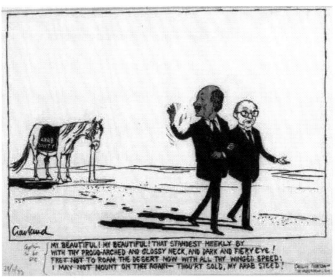

Nicholas Garland, Courtesy the New Statesman, November 25th, 1977

Jimmy Carter and Camp David

Jimmy Carter showed during the Camp David Accords his firmness as well as his sense of caring for the welfare of both sides. He brought Egypt's President Sadat and Israel Prime Minister Begin to come to an agreement that seemed impossible to achieve. During the Iranian hostage crisis, he stayed focused, poised and calm. He was accused of not being close to the Washington establishments with a tendency to micro manage.

Dr. Ucynski believed a number of Presidents had low emotional intelligence. Richard Nixon, in her view, was paranoid and kept grudges. He did not have an easy good humor or the social skills of most politicians. He was demanding and often disregarded the feelings of others, in her opinion. Lyndon Johnson was energetic but compulsive and manipulative and could be deceptive and cunning to a fault. Johnson, like Nixon, often viewed criticism as persona attacks. Clinton was brilliant but lacked self-discipline. Hoover, Coolidge and Wilson, she relates, were different types of leaders but shared an introverted nature. This worked against their effectiveness. Instead of appearing outgoing and friendly, they were seen as austere and cold and "sometimes easily irritated and overwhelmed by stress."[104]

Franklin Roosevelt's Fatal Secret

Last know photo of Franklin Roosevelt, on the afternoon of April 11th, 1945. He died the next day.
Courtesy National Archives

---

[104] Ibid Posten http://www2.readingeagle.com/article.aspx?id=125717

In 2011, newspaper reports came out concerning a seven decade old letter about the health of Franklin Delano Roosevelt while he was campaigning for the Presidency for an unprecedented fourth time. On July 10th, 1944, Dr. Frank Lahey, Chairman of the Directing Board, for Physicians, Dentists and Veterinarians of the War Manpower Commission of the Office of Emergency Management wrote a confidential memo citing his objections and concerns about the health of the President.

Dr. Frank Lahey, Courtesy National Archives

Lahey was a prominent doctor and surgeon. He had personally examined the President and recorded his findings and discussed them with FDR, directly. He recommended he not seek a fourth term and that if he did to find an appropriate Vice President to succeed him. This information was also made aware to Democratic Party leaders who would select the candidate for the 1944 Presidential election.

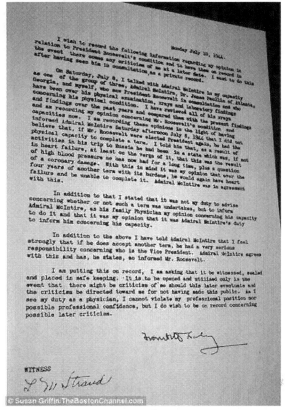

Dr. Frank Lahey's Letter of July 10th, 1944, Courtesy Lahey Clinic

The President's health had been declining for years. The stress of the job laid heavily on his shoulders. It had effected his entire being and was now snuffing out his life. Franklin Roosevelt knew he was going to die. He knew he would not finish his last term in office. As a result, he changed Vice Presidents and chose a little know Senator from Missouri named Harry S. Truman who Party leaders believed was capable to succeed FDR.[105]

---

[105] Daniel Bates, Mail Online, April 11th, 2011
Memo Warned Franklin D. Roosevelt he would Die if he ran for a Fourth Term

Dr. Lahey had examined the President. He felt it was necessary to go on record and explain his diagnosis in the event that someone someday would question it. The President was informed, in July, 1944, that he was going to die, according to Dr. Lahey's letter. The Doctor predicted that Roosevelt would be gone within a year. He died ten months later from a massive stroke. Steven Lomazow, co-author of *FDR's Deadly Secret* stated: "It is quite evident that FDR was well aware of his diagnosis and prognosis prior to accepting the Democratic nomination for the president."

Questions circulated during the start of the Fourth term as to FDR's physical and mental health and his ability to continue as President. Franklin Roosevelt's travelling Secretary, William D. Hassett, recorded this in his diary of March 30th, 1945:[106]

"FDR returned from the 14,000 mile trip to the Yalta Conference on February 28, 1945. The next day, he appeared before a Joint Session of Congress to report on the conference. His delivery of the speech was erratic, and he made frequent rambling departures from the written text. The President remained in Washington until March 24, when he went home to Hyde Park for a few days. He returned to Washington on March 29 for a day, and then continued on to Warm Springs. Everyone hoped that Warm Springs would rejuvenate the President, as it had always done before."

The President was logically exhausted from the voyage. He mentioned it in his remarks to the Congress: "I hope that you will pardon me for this unusual posture of sitting down during the presentation of what I want to say, but I know that you will realize

---

[106] FDR's Health, Diary of Presidential Secretary William D. Hassett, March 30th, 1945.http://www.fdrlibraryvirtualtour.org/graphics/07-38/7.5_FDRs_Health.pdf

that it makes it a lot easier for me not to have to carry about ten pounds of steel around on the bottom of my legs; and also because of the fact that I have just completed a fourteen-thousand-mile trip."
107

Rumors spread about his inability to act coherently in Yalta. These raised concerns from those nearest the President.
Hassett later recorded in his diary: "He is slipping away and no earthly power can keep him here...To all the staff, to the family and with the Boss himself I have maintained the bluff; but I am convinced that there is no help for him." Franklin Roosevelt died in Warm Springs, Georgia thirteen days later.

In releasing the letter of Dr. Lahey, Dr. John Libertino, director of the Lahey Clinic's Sophia Gordon Cancer Center stated:

"The real issue is: There is a delicate balance between patient confidentiality and national security. Both issues were in play at the time, so some may view this as a conspiracy, as have some authors. But when you consider the circumstances of the country at the time, it was probably either a political or heroic act by FDR."[108]

Thus, the key question to be faced is should a President be allowed to continue in office if his health is failing? Woodrow Wilson was incapacitated with a stroke in the last year of his Administration. John Kennedy's had severe health problems. The public has a right to know not only if the President is physically and mentally capable to continue the job but also if a candidate for President is fit to take

[107] The Miller Center of the University of Virginia, Address to Congress on Yalta, March 1st, 1945 http://millercenter.org/president/fdroosevelt/speeches/speech-3338

[108] Carey Goldberg, Long-Lost 'Lahey Memo' On FDR's Health Unveiled, Common Health, April 8th, 2 http://commonhealth.wbur.org/2011/04/what-killed-fdr

on the awesome burden of President of the United States, physically and mentally.

Imagine the critical moments and trials our new government will confront in 2016. Our new President must have nerves of steel. There will be moments that test America's will and pride like what to do in the Middle East as radicals continue to expand their deadly reach? Who will have the strength, courage and wisdom to deal with another attack on America like 9-11? Who can we trust to protect us and the world from nuclear war? Who will make decisions based on facts and not emotion? The answers are why the right choice of a President in 2016 is so vital.

Chapter Eight: Courage and Wisdom

It is not the critic who counts: not the man who points out how the strong man stumbles or where the doer of deeds could have done them better. The credit belongs to the man who is actually in the arena, whose face is marred by dust and sweat and blood, who strives valiantly, who errs and comes up short again and again ... who spends himself in a worthy cause; who, at the best, knows, in the end, the triumph of high achievement, and who at the worst, if he fails, at least he fails while daring greatly. **Theodore Roosevelt**

You gain strength, courage, and confidence by every experience in which you really stop to look fear in the face. You are able to say to yourself, 'I lived through this horror. I can take the next thing that comes along.' **Eleanor Roosevelt**

I learned that courage was not the absence of fear, but the triumph over it. The brave man is not he who does not feel afraid, but he who conquers that fear. **Nelson Mandela**

God grant me the serenity to accept the things I cannot change, the courage to change the things I can, and the wisdom to know the difference. **Reinhold Niebuhr**

In whatever arena of life one may meet the challenge of courage, whatever may be the sacrifices he faces if he follows his conscience – the loss of his friends, his fortune, his contentment, even the esteem of his fellow men – each man must decide for himself the course he will follow. **John F. Kennedy**

A President must bring courage and wisdom to the Office. It cannot be acquired later. It is part of their character and temperament. It is the reason why he or she is there. Courage requires sacrifice and risk. Political courage means taking a stand based on principle, no matter what the consequences. It demands doing the right thing for the people of the United States and the world even if, at that moment, it appears to be the wrong decision at the wrong time. Such was the case when Gerald Ford pardoned Richard Nixon.

Gerald Ford is sworn in as the 38th President of the United States by Chief Justice Warren Burger in the White House East Room on August 9th, 1974, Courtesy National Archives

Gerald Ford and the Nixon Pardon

On September 8th, 1974, President Gerald Ford pardoned his predecessor, Richard Nixon. It was one of the most controversial Presidential actions in history. Nixon was on the verge of being indicted for the cover up dealing with the Watergate scandal. He resigned. Less than a month after he took the oath of office, Ford pardoned his predecessor "for all offenses against the United States which he, Richard Nixon, has committed or may have committed or taken part in during the period from January 20, 1969 through August 9, 1974."[109] Ford knew that history would judge him for this act. He explained to the people why he felt that it was necessary. "It is believed that a trial of Richard Nixon, if it became necessary, could not fairly begin until a year or more has elapsed. In the meantime, the tranquility to which this nation has been restored by the events of recent weeks could be irreparably lost by the prospects of bringing to trial a former President of the United States." Ford was a man of compassion. He added these words to the pardon: "I feel that Richard Nixon and his loved ones have suffered enough."[110]

Ford viewed Watergate as an "American tragedy" which needed to be ended. He knew he was the only one who had the power to do so. With the Nixon pardon, "our long national nightmare" would be concluded, he said. [111] His chief concern was to move ahead with the country's business without the burden Richard Nixon's trial interfering with the national agenda. Vietnam and the economy were high priority problems that needed the undivided attention of the President of the United States and the Congress.

Ford was almost universally criticized for the pardon. It was a factor that cost him the election of 1976. Forty years after the Nixon pardon, those who were among Ford's harshest critics gathered and looked back at the event. Carl Bernstein and Bob Woodward were the Washington Post reporters who uncovered the Watergate

[109] Text of President Ford's Pardon Proclamation, September 08, 1974, http://watergate.info/1974/09/08/text-of-ford-pardon-proclamation.html

[74] Caroline Kennedy, Profiles in Courage for Our Time, John F. Kennedy Library Foundation, Boston, 2001, p. 295

scandal. They vehemently criticized Ford at the time. Four decades later, Woodward called the pardon "an act of courage." Bernstein said it took "great courage." Senator Edward Kennedy acknowledged that it was in the best interests of the country. Watergate Prosecutor, Richard Ben-Veniste took it even further: [112]

The decision to pardon Nixon was a political judgment properly within the bounds of Ford's constitutional authority...Jerry Ford acted in accord with what he sincerely felt were the best interests of the country; that there was no secret quid pro quo with Nixon for a pardon in return for resignation; and that Ford, a compassionate man, was moved by the palpable suffering of a man who had lost so much.

Caroline Kennedy said of him: "Ford's ambition for the country was larger than his own ambition. Restored confidence was more important than his reelection. That's courage."[113]

---

[112] The Nixon pardon in retrospect, 40 years later, September 8, 2014 by the National Constitutional Center, *http://blog.constitutioncenter.org/2014/09/the-nixon-pardon-in-retrospect-40-years-later/*

[113] Ibid Caroline Kennedy, p.314-315

Franklin Roosevelt with Ruthie Bie and Fala at Hilltop Cottage in Hyde Park, 1941, Courtesy
Franklin Delano Roosevelt Library

Franklin Roosevelt and Polio

In 1921, Franklin Delano Roosevelt was considered one of the
bright lights of the Democrat Party and a future Presidential
contender. He had gone to the best schools. He was an
accomplished public speaker. He was handsome, charming,
charismatic and witty. He was former Assistant Secretary of the
Navy and Vice Presidential candidate in 1920. Franklin was the
cousin of Teddy Roosevelt, one of the most popular leaders in
American history.

Like Teddy, he came from a family of wealth and influence. His was a star truly on the rise. Then, in the summer of 1921, polio struck. Infantile paralysis became the greatest personal and political hurdle in his life. His illness made the headlines of the New York Times. Many thought that his political career was over. Franklin Roosevelt believed this as well. No one in his condition had been elected to high political office in American history.

Louie Howe with FDR in 1932, Courtesy Library of Congress

Two people had faith in him: Eleanor Roosevelt and Louie Howe. Eleanor knew he had the inner strength to overcome his infirmity. Howe was his top political adviser. He saw greatness in Franklin Roosevelt and believed that he would muster the political courage to return to public life. It took FDR three years. He found some relief in the waters of a resort in Warm Springs, Georgia. Most of all, he found hope.

It was the hope that he could someday walk again that propelled Franklin Roosevelt forward. It was an inner voice that told him that he could persevere and return to advance his political career despite infantile paralysis. It took enormous courage for Roosevelt to take the first steps to rehabilitate himself in the eyes of his Party and the eyes of the public.

FDR used crutches when nominating Al Smith at the 1924 Democratic National Convention, the speech that marked his return to public life, June 26th, 1924, Courtesy Franklin Delano Roosevelt Library

The great opportunity came during the Presidential convention of 1924. Roosevelt was asked to put in nomination the name of Alfred E. Smith, Governor of New York for President of the United States.

The following passage from *Profiles in Leadership from Caesar to Modern* times describes Roosevelt's anxiety and how he overcame his fear with the courage of his wife:[114]

"FDR was frightened. He feared his paralysis would cause him to lose control, fall during the convention and show he did not have the stamina to be a leader. Eleanor helped him meet the challenge. She encouraged him. She relieved his fears. She said later, that polio taught Franklin what suffering was about. His illness made him stronger.

Even though he was paralyzed from the waist down, and could not move his legs, steel braces helped hold him erect. He learned to toss his lower body out one leg at a time to give the impression of walking while holding on to the arm of his son. Finally, convinced he could succeed, FDR offered to put the Governor's name in nomination at the 1924 Democratic Presidential Convention. Smith was delighted.

It was late June. New York was sweltering. Over a thousand of party members huddled into the hot stands of a Madison Square Garden. At the Garden, FDR entered through a back door. He wanted to avoid reporters taking photos of him in a wheel chair. He was carried up the stairs, thrown over the back of a strong aide. Behind a curtain, he took up his crutches. He was perspiring. His family was in the wings watching and waiting. William J. Vanden Heuvel described what followed:

On the arm of his son FDR, with his legs firm in locked braces, holding a cane in his other hand, advanced slowly without crutches to the podium in Madison Square Garden. It was a moment that no one who saw it would ever forget. His palpable courage, his lyrical eloquence, his magnificent voice, brought the delegates to their feet – and at that moment Franklin Roosevelt resumed a national

---

[114] Emilio Iodice, Profiles in Leadership from Caesar to Modern Times, North American Business Press, Miami, Florida, 2013, p. 285

political career. Seven years after his polio attack Roosevelt was elected Governor of New York. As Frank Freidel, one of the important Roosevelt biographers has written, Roosevelt had perfected so effective an illusion of his strength and wellbeing that most Americans never realized until after his death that he was, in fact, a paraplegic.

The crowd, spell bound, heard FDR call Smith, 'The Happy Warrior.' After one hundred and three ballots, John W. Davis, former Congressman from West Virginia was selected. Smith lost the nomination. Calvin Coolidge won another term in office by a landslide. In spite of the election outcome, Franklin and Eleanor Roosevelt had a personal and political triumph. It would carry them to the Governor's mansion and to the White House."

Ticket to a 1935 "Birthday Ball" honoring President Franklin Roosevelt. Courtesy Franklin Delano Roosevelt Library

Eleanor Roosevelt, Courtesy the White House

During his Presidency, Franklin Roosevelt worked to raise funds to help the disabled and conduct research for a polio vaccine. Each year, a birthday party would be held in his honor to help the cause. Thanks to him and Eleanor, the March of Dimes was created. On April 12, 1955, the tenth anniversary of the death of FDR, the first results of the successful field test of the Salk vaccine was announced.

Franklin Roosevelt, 1941, Courtesy Franklin Delano Roosevelt Library

Seventeen years after Franklin Roosevelt put the name of Al Smith before the Democrat Convention, he faced another challenge that demanded courage and wisdom. On January 10th, 1941, President Roosevelt introduced Lend-Lease to the US Congress. The Battle of Britain was raging. The United Kingdom could fall to Nazi Germany at any time. FDR knew that America was the "last bastion of democracy" to help England survive the Nazi onslaught. Lend-Lease permitted military aid to any nation whose security was vital to the United States. It gave the President the power to "lend" arms to Britain with the accord that the US would be repaid in kind after the war. Staunch isolationists opposed the plan. FDR mustered all the political influence and courage at his disposal to get the law passed. It was accepted by the Congress overwhelmingly. The plan gave the United States time to prepare for the rising threat from Japan and Germany. It helped organize our military and navy for a two front war which would be the greatest challenge America would ever face.

Little boy receiving a pair of shoes in Europe after the War, Courtesy George C. Marshall Foundation

Franklin Roosevelt's vision, courage and political skill starting with Lend-Lease laid the foundation for the post war period and the Marshall Plan to feed the starving millions after with War and rebuild Europe and Japan.

FDR and the Holocaust

"Progressives have a long and admirable record of honestly acknowledging FDR's failings alongside his achievements. Roosevelt's response to the Holocaust is no more defensible than his internment of Japanese-Americans or his troubling record on the rights of African-Americans. Recognizing that fact does not endanger the legacy of the New Deal or diminish FDR's accomplishments in bringing America out of the Depression or his leadership in World War II. It merely acknowledges his flaws as well." These are the words of Rafael Medoff, Founding Director of the David S. Wyman Institute for Holocaust Studies in a September, 2013 article in The Nation entitled *FDR and the Holocaust* by Lawrence Zuckerman.

Arial reconnaissance photograph of Auschwitz showing Auschwits II (Birkenau) taken by the U.S. Air Force between April 4, 1944 and January 15, 1945. (USHMM Photo Archive).

It is clear that the Allies knew of the Nazi extermination program at the outset of World War II. In an April, 2015 article entitled, *Auschwitz Bombing Controversy: Could the Allies Have Bombed Auschwitz-Birkenau?* by Mitchell Bard, in the Jewish Virtual Library, evidence is presented of detailed information about the camps from survivors in 1942. They exhibited data about the mass exterminations and explained how the camps could be bombed and destroyed to stop the killings.

Former Senator George McGovern, a bomber pilot in World War II, stated that his squadron hit Nazi oil facilities less than five miles from Auschwitz. He said in 2005: "There is no question we should have attempted to go after Auschwitz. There was a pretty good chance we could have blasted those rail lines off the face of the earth, which would have interrupted the flow of people to those death chambers, and we had a pretty good chance of knocking out those gas ovens."

At the height of the Holocaust, in 1943, one of FDR's staunchest supporters, journalist Freda Kirchwey, denounced his failure to respond to Nazi genocide. She wrote, "You and I and the President and the Congress and the State Department are accessories to the crime and share Hitler's guilt," she wrote. "If we had behaved like humane and generous people instead of complacent, cowardly ones, the two million Jews lying today in the earth of Poland and Hitler's other crowded graveyards would be alive and safe.... We had it in our power to rescue this doomed people and we did not lift a hand to do it—or perhaps it would be fairer to say that we lifted just one cautious hand, encased in a tight-fitting glove of quotas and visas and affidavits, and a thick layer of prejudice."

Kirchwey was editor of *The Nation,* a magazine which, as early as 1938, called for the US to rescue Jews after the Kristallnacht when it was clear that millions were in danger. The publication asked for the rescue of 15,000 German Jewish refugee children. The Roosevelt Administration refused. Kirchwey wrote in 1940: "The Roosevelt administration's refugee policy is one which must sicken any person of ordinarily humane instinct. It is as if we were to examine laboriously the curriculum vitae of flood victims clinging to a piece of floating wreckage and finally to decide that no matter what their virtues, all but a few had better be allowed to drown."

Franklin Roosevelt was presented with information about the "Final Solution" by his advisers shortly after the US entered the War. FDR's Secretary of the Treasury and one of his most trusted aides,

Henry Morgenthau, said that the US knew of the camps in 1942, according to Michael Beschloss in his 2002 book, *The Conquerors. Roosevelt, Truman and the Destruction of Hitler's Germany, 1941-1945,* (Simon and Shuster). Morgenthau tried to persuade FDR to take action but failed. Secretary of War Henry L. Stimson opposed any measures as did the Assistant Secretary of War, John J. McCoy and Secretary of State Cordell Hull.

Beschloss says the Allies failed to deliver "a moral statement for all time that the British and Americans understood the historical gravity of the Holoucast." Roosevelt refused Morgenthau's repeated exhortations to bomb Auschwitz. Beschloss argues that FDR remained "shockingly disengaged from the struggle to rescue Jewish refugees from Hitler." He did not try "to explore whether death camps bombings and transportation lines might have saved lives."

Franklin Roosevelt was the most powerful national leader in World War II. He had the power to stop one of the most brutal crimes the world has ever seen. It is an example of the ability of the President of the United States to change the course of history and fight evil or allow it to continue on its path of destruction and anguish.

Last known photograph of Lincoln taken by Henry F. Warren on the White House balcony, March 6, 1865.
Courtesy Library of Congress

Lincoln and Slavery

By the end of the Civil War, Abraham Lincoln had repeatedly demonstrated physical, mental and political courage far beyond any of our Presidents before or after him. He endured constant pressure from Cabinet members, political opponents, members of his Party and the press. He faced assassination threats. He battled with military officials over the course of the war. He constantly changed generals and officers until he found General Grant. He showed bravery in issuing the Emancipation Proclamation. His closest advisers were against it. They warned him that he would lose re-election if he issued the Proclamation. Radical Republicans and

War Democrats opposed him. He stuck to his convictions.[115] The Emancipation Proclamation was signed on January 1st, 1863. It did not immediately end slavery but laid the groundwork for passage of the 13th Amendment to the Constitution permanently ending slavery.

Currier and Ives, 1865

One of Lincoln's last acts of political courage was his Second Inaugural Address on March 4th, 1865. The War was ending. He could have cited his amazing achievements in bringing the nation to victory, eliminating slavery and preserving the Union. He did not. Instead, Abraham Lincoln removed himself from any accomplishments and offered questions as to why the conflict happened to begin with. He searched into the conscience of

---

[115] Michael Beschloss, Presidential Courage: Brave Leaders and How They Changed America 1789-1989, by Michael Beschloss, Simon & Schuster, May 2007, as quoted in the book review online on America's Trust http://americastrust.us/presidentialcourage.html

America to reflect on what had happened and what would now confront the nation.

He realized that many who were listening wanted revenge against the South. The people of the North blamed the South for starting the War. They blamed them for the bloodshed and suffering. Many wanted retribution. Abraham Lincoln wanted forgiveness. He asked for charity, compassion and "to care for him who shall have borne the battle, and for his widow, and his orphan." Lincoln was not seeking political correctness in lauding the victories of the North. He was asking for mercy for the vanquished, "With Malice toward none, with charity for all, with firmness in the right, as God gives us to see the right, let us strive on to finish the work we are in, to bind up the nation's wounds." It was a wonderful show of courage and wisdom.[116]

---

[116] Ted Widmer, And the End Came, New York Times, March 3rd, 2015

Ford's Theatre, the night of Friday, April 14, 1865, Courtesy National Archives

His final act came a month and eleven days later when a member of the audience who listened to him on that chilly March day, John Wilkes Booth, shot him on April 14th, 1865 while watching a play in Ford's Theatre in Washington, DC. Abraham Lincoln died the next day.

For this Presidential election we need a Lincoln. We require the wisdom and courage to do the right thing, even if it is not the right time. The situations will arise during the term of the next occupant of the White House which will test his or her bravery, compassion and good judgment.

History, despite its wrenching pain, cannot be unlived, but if faced with courage, need not be lived again. **Maya Angelou**

Whatever you do, you need courage. Whatever course you decide upon, there is always someone to tell you that you are wrong. There are always difficulties arising that tempt you to believe your critics are right. To map out a course of action and follow it to an end requires some of the same courage that a soldier needs. Peace has its victories, but it takes brave men and women to win them.

Ralph Waldo Emerson

Whatever we learn to do, we learn by actually doing it; men come to be builders, for instance, by building, and harp players by playing the harp. In the same way, by doing just acts we come to be just; by doing self-controlled acts, we come to be self-controlled; and by doing brave acts, we become brave. **Aristotle**

Chapter Nine: Decision Maker

Never cut a tree down in the wintertime. Never make a negative decision in the low time. Never make your most important decisions when you are in your worst moods. Wait. Be patient. The storm will pass. The spring will come. **Robert H. Schuller**

It is difficult for the common good to prevail against the intense concentration of those who have a special interest, especially if the decisions are made behind locked doors. Jimmy Carter

It is very important to know who you are. To make decisions. To show who you are. **Malala Yousafzai**

I am always wary of decisions made hastily. I am always wary of the first decision, that is, the first thing that comes to my mind if I have to make a decision. This is usually the wrong thing. I have to wait and assess, looking deep into myself, taking the necessary time. **Pope Francis**

Making good decisions is a crucial skill at every level. **Peter Drucker**

I think that we must find some way to get more common sense, more rationality, in our decisions and less emotion. **David Packard**

All our final decisions are made in a state of mind that is not going to last. **Marcel Proust**

Exceptionally hard decisions can deplete your energy to the point at which you finally cave in. If you mentally crumble and

degenerate into negative thinking, you'll magnify the problem to the point where it can haunt you. **John C. Maxwell**

At the essence of the American Presidency is decision-making. Nothing may be more important than a President's ability to make good decisions. They shape history, bring us war or peace or economic growth or stagnation. Presidential choices impact the nation for generations. The style, skill and experience a candidate has in making decisions should factor heavily in the choice for our country's highest office.

Lincoln Selecting General Grant, "The Old Bull Dog," after relieving General McClellan Courtesy Library of Congress

The Presidency: The Buck Stops Here

Abraham Lincoln, for example, was in the telegraph room of the White House, nearly every day. There, he got the latest information on the battles won and lost in the Civil War. He asked questions, searched for data and truth, before making the life and death decisions he constantly faced. Excellent leaders are able to simplify a dilemma with evidence. They are not afraid to decide. Harry Truman said, "The buck stops here."[117]

During the early part of the Obama administration, journalist Jonathan Alter did a study of decision making by President Barack Obama. Alter devoted a considerable amount of time, energy and research in studying the style of how the new President made decisions. John W. Dean analyzed Alter's findings in a 2010 article for Final Law. [118] Dean was White House Counsel for President Nixon from 1970 to 1973. He was deeply involved in the events leading up to the Watergate burglary and the cover-up. The FBI referred to Dean as the "master manipulator of the cover-up." He turned state's evidence and was a key witness for the prosecution. Dean served a reduced prison sentence for his collaboration which ultimately resulted in the end of the Nixon Presidency.[119]

Dean said Obama's style falls between that of George W. Bush and Bill Clinton. Bush had an intuitive style of decision making. It was based on instinct and "gut feel," instead of relying on his Cabinet, staff and professionals who could provide facts for logical and rational judgements. According to Dean, the result of Bush's way of making decisions led to the disasters in Iraq and Afghanistan and the damage to the American economy that may take decades to heal.

[117] Emilio Iodice, Profiles in Leadership from Caesar to Modern Time, North American Business Press, Miami, 2013, p.294

[118] How our Decider-in-Chief Decides: Decision Making in the Obama Presidency, John W. Dean, Final Law, April 6th 2010 http://writ.news.findlaw.com/dean/20100806.html, Jonathan Alter, The Promise, President Obama, Year One, Simon and Schuster, New York, 2010

[119] Office of Planning and Evaluation (July 5, 1974). "FBI Watergate Investigation: OPE Analysis" (PDF). Federal Bureau of Investigation. p. 11. File Number 139-4089. Retrieved July 19, 2011.

2016 Selecting the President

"Clinton was an inductive thinker with a horizontal mind. He talked to people in wide-ranging college bull sessions (or late at night on the phone) to establish a broad array of policy and political options, then looked at them in context and fashioned a synthetic and often brilliant political approach out of the tangled strands of analysis."[120] Obama, instead, makes decisions in the same style he used in law school when he headed the *Harvard Law Review*.

Obama is a "deductive" thinker with a vertical way of reasoning. He reflects profoundly about a subject and fashions it in a point-by-point series of arguments. He wants memos that lay out clear policy options. He prefers logic to imagination, in Alter's view. While Clinton constantly reviewed and second guessed his choices, Obama decides and moves on unless something out of the ordinary requires going back to re-evaluate the situation.[121]

He wants all available data about a subject. He probes his agencies and staffs and "encourages dissent rather than yes-people." Obama listens carefully. He repeats what he has heard to make sure he has grasped the fundamentals and has interpreted the arguments accurately. He encourages his team to think in terms of a larger vision and "the big picture" vs. getting swamped in details. He changes his approach to problem solving so that his staff is kept off-balance and does not tell him what they think he wants to hear. Obama does not make believe he understands when he does not. He asks questions. At the close of a meeting, he summarizes what has been said, decides and ends the discussion.

Dean and Alter believe the approach Obama follows is an example of the way choices should be made in the White House. Rarely have Presidents worked this way, they contend. John Kennedy

---

120 Ibid. Dean
121 Ibid. Dean

failed in making sound decisions in the Bay of Pigs invasion but got it right, in their view, during the Cuban Missile Crisis.

Dean feels Obama is writing the "textbook" on proper Presidential decision making. Even so, he brings up an important question. Is his style devoid of emotion? He is remarkably cool when tackling crises. He constantly remains self-confident and focused. Clinton was subject to "purple fits" and tantrums. Bush went with his gut feel. Obama acts calmly and logically. He stays in control of his emotions and, as a result, maintains control of the emotions of those around him. He realizes that this is not always the best approach but he prefers it to any other. Dean believes Obama may be one of our better decision makers because of his style and fact based method to tackling difficult choices.

Obama's former CIA Director, Leon Panetta challenged this view. He was head of the intelligence agency from 2009 to 2011. In his book, *Worthy Fights,* Panetta criticized the President's style of making decisions. [122] Panetta argued against declassifying information related to the Bush-era interrogation tactics, for example. Obama overruled him. Panetta disagreed: "it seemed wrong to me to ask a public servant to take a risk for his country and assure him that it was both legal and approved, then, years later, to suggest that he had done something wrong." Panetta viewed this incident as part of the pattern of how Obama made decisions. In his view, Obama's manner was too "insular." Decision-making was conducted with the President's inner circle of staffers, often bypassing the Cabinet and the counsel of senior advisers and experts. The failure to consult specialists, according to Panetta, damaged the administration's ability to explain problems and their solutions. Non-political challenges became political with Obama's

---

[122] Panetta's Memoir Blasts Obama On His Leadership, Blames Him For State Of Iraq And Syria ,By Lauren Walker, Newsweek, October 10th, 2011.

form of making decisions. Obama, believed Panetta, had a "disdain for Congress," refusing to allow agency heads to deliberate with members.

Perhaps Panetta's biggest criticism is the drawdown in Iraq. He insisted that leaving a modest force would preserve stability and reduce the chances of terrorism. The administration wanted to end an unpopular war which they did not support even if the head of the CIA and the Joint Chiefs of Staff and military commanders felt differently. The resurgence of Al Qaeda and now ISIS arises from those critical decisions, in the eyes of administration detractors.

Henry Kissinger being sworn in as Secretary of State by Chief Justice Warren Burger, September 22, 1973. Kissinger's mother, Paula, holds the Bible upon which he was sworn in while President Nixon looks on, Courtesy National Archives

Mao and Nixon Playing "Ping Pong Diplomacy 1972, Courtesy the Presidency and the Cold War

Another critic was former Defense Secretary Robert Gates. "His White House was by far the most centralized and controlling in national security of any I had seen since Richard Nixon and Henry Kissinger ruled the roost,"[123] Gates writes in a recent memoir. He felt "blindsided" at times by decisions made at White House that affected defense. He considered Obama a man of integrity but questioned his ability to make sound judgements regarding national security.

---

[123] Reuters, Janruary 7th, 2014, Former U.S. Defense Secretary Gates criticizes Obama in memoir, http://www.reuters.com/article/2014/01/08/us-usa-gates-obama-idUSBREA0618020140108

Other Presidents faced challenges that required tough decisions that affected our history. Presidents like Adams and Jefferson had fewer staff resources to assist them than modern Presidents but still had to make historic choices.

John Adams, Courtesy the White House

John Adams: Keeping us out of War with France

The second President of the United States, John Adams, was known for his strong personality and independent decision making. Adams was criticized for his temper and demeanor which could be very argumentative. He admitted that he lacked patience and did not suffer fools silently.[124]

---

[124] George C. Herring, (2008). From colony to superpower: U.S. foreign relations since 1776. Oxford University Press, p. 91

Like his predecessor, George Washington, Adams was considered a patriot of good character, and promoter of republican values. He kept Washington's Cabinet to permit a smoother succession. They were often hostile to his decisions which, at times, he made without consulting them. Thomas Jefferson was Vice President. Adams' Cabinet was led by a team loyal to Alexander Hamilton who felt a small aristocratic group with ties to England should lead the country, even if it led to war with France. Britain and France were at war. Many Americans recalled that France had helped in the Revolutionary War and were sympathetic to the French. Adams felt that the young republic needed to avoid European entanglements at all cost, even if it meant he would not be re-elected. Adam's self-reliance kept us out of war.

When the French began seizing US merchant vessels, Adams fortified the Navy and defied the French by harassing their vessels on the high seas. He strengthened the army to prevent an invasion. Adams signed the Alien and Sedition Act which levied penalties on foreigners who spoke out against the government. It angered his political enemies and the public at large. In February, 1799, he sent an emissary to France to negotiate with Napoleon. It led to an end to conflict and signaled the start of friendly relations. John Adams avoided war but lost his bid for re-election.

Adams felt that one of his greatest achievements was keeping America from going to war with France. He and Thomas Jefferson died on the same day, July 4th, 1826. [125] He asked the following to be written on his tombstone: "Here lies John Adams, who took upon himself the responsibility of peace with France in the year 1800."

---

[125] McCullough, John (2001). John Adams. Simon & Schuster. p. 622

Abraham Lincoln, Courtesy Library of Congress

Abraham Lincoln and the Attack on Fort Sumter

As Abraham Lincoln was about to assume office, he faced a crisis beyond expectations. The United States was being torn apart by secessionism. It began on an island in the harbor of Charleston bay. South Carolina seceded from the Union on December 20th, 1860. On Christmas day, 68 federal troops stationed in Charleston withdrew to Fort Sumter. The North considered the fort to be federal property. South Carolina insisted that it was part of the newly formed Confederate States of America. In February, 1861, Jefferson Davis was inaugurated provisional President of the Confederacy. One month later, Abraham Lincoln took the oath of office.

Fort Sumter, Courtesy Library of Congress

Within weeks he faced one of the most crucial decisions of his life. Fort Sumter was circled by South Carolina militia. The only way to supply the Fort was by attacking the militia. This would be an act of war and considered Northern aggression. There were states that had still not seceded. If the North liberated the Fort, it might drive other states into the hands of the Confederacy. Foreign powers might take sides to support the South. At the same time, he could not permit his troops to starve or surrender and risk showing weakness. Lincoln met with his Cabinet and advisers and military leaders and studied all options and possible outcomes. He could withdraw the troops from Fort Sumter and negotiate with the South. He could use the Fort to launch an invasion and forcibly bring the South back into the Union. He settled on a middle course that left his options opened.

Jefferson Finis Davis, President of the Confederate States, Courtesy National Archives

On April 6th, Lincoln sent a message to the governor of South Carolina. He said he would send provisions to Fort Sumter but no arms, troops or ammunition unless South Carolina attacked. The decision now rested with Jefferson Davis. If the South attacked the Northern troops supplying the Fort, they would be the aggressors. Davis could not permit the Fort to be resupplied. He ordered Major Anderson, Commander of Fort Sumter to surrender. He refused. "The Civil War began at 4:30 a.m. on April 12, 1861, when Confederate artillery, under the command of General Pierre Gustave T. Beauregard, opened fire on Fort Sumter. Confederate batteries showered the fort with over 3,000 shells in a three-and-a-half day period. Anderson surrendered. Ironically, Beauregard had developed his military skills under Anderson's instruction at West Point. This was the first of countless relationships and families devastated in the Civil War. The fight was on."[126]

---

[126] US History.org, Fort Sumter, http://www.ushistory.org/us/33a.asp

The attack on Fort Sumter portrayed the North as the victim and not the aggressor. It helped Lincoln rally popular support for what would be the bloodiest conflict in American history.

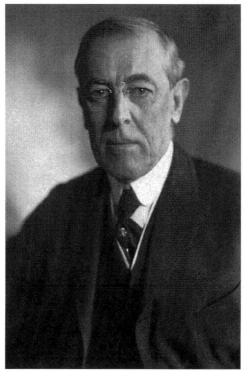

Woodrow Wilson, Courtesy Library of Congress

Woodrow Wilson: The Decision to Go to War

"He Kept us Out of War." This was the slogan that helped re-elect Woodrow Wilson to the White House in 1916. The War in Europe began two years earlier. The United States declared its neutrality even in the face of unrestricted submarine warfare on the part of Germany. Wilson promised to keep the United States from being entangled in a war that was taking on global proportions. He did not want to be forced to change his stand. A year before the 1916 campaign, an event happened that enraged the American public against Germany.

RMS Lusitania, 1915, Courtesy Library of Congress

The passenger ship, *Lusitania,* set sail on May 1st, 1915 from New York bound for Liverpool. It had nearly 2000 passengers. It was the fastest ship afloat. The day before it set sail, its captain, William Turner, testified in an ongoing investigation of the Titanic sinking. He knew details about the treacherous conditions of the Irish Sea and the North Atlantic. What he did not know was that German submarines were prowling the waters in search of British prey.

Below the decks of the Lusitania, were tons of munitions bound for the United Kingdom.[127] The Admiralty had mounted turrets for guns on the luxury liner. Seven days into its voyage, German submarine U 20 launched a torpedo. It was 2:10 PM on May 7. Two explosions rocked the vessel. The first came from the torpedo and the second from an unknown source. The ship sank in 18

---

[127] http://www.eyewitnesstohistory.com/snpwwi2.htm, The Sinking of the Lusitania

minutes. 1,119 passengers died including 114 Americans. A firestorm of protest against Germany occurred. President Wilson sent a strong protest to the Kaiser. US Secretary of State William Jennings Bryan was a pacifist. He resigned realizing that war was up ahead.

This cartoon, featuring President Woodrow Wilson, was in response to continued German U-boat attacks at sea in World War I. (March, 21, 1917), Courtesy National Archives

Less than two years later, the Germans attempted an alliance with Mexico that forced Woodrow Wilson to reconsider America's neutrality. British authorities gave the US a telegram from German Foreign Secretary Arthur Zimmerman to the German Ambassador to Mexico. It proposed a German-Mexican alliance in the event of war with the United States. Germany promised Mexico restoration of the territories lost to the US during the Mexican War of 1845. The telegram appeared on the front pages of newspapers around the world on March 1st, 1917. At first it was suspected of being a hoax.

Two days later, Zimmerman revealed that it was true. Americans were horrified. Wilson could no longer wait. He had to decide on the only course of action.

On April 2nd, President Wilson asked for a declaration of war. It was approved four days later. He asked the American people to join the fight "to make the world safe for democracy."

The Manhattan Project

It was August 2nd, 1939. Albert Einstein was teaching at Princeton University. On that date, he wrote an historic letter to President Franklin Delano Roosevelt one month before the German attack on Poland that started World War II. It would change the course of history.

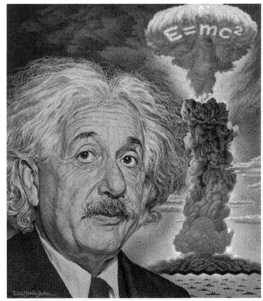

Albert Einstein, Cover of Time Magazine, 1946, Courtesy Time

He said to FDR:

"….it may become possible to set up a nuclear chain reaction in a large mass of uranium, by which vast amounts of power and large quantities of new radium-like elements would be generated. Now it appears almost certain that this could be achieved in the immediate future. This new phenomenon would also lead to the construction of bombs, and it is conceivable - though much less certain - that extremely powerful bombs of a new type may thus be constructed. A single bomb of this type, carried by boat and exploded in a port, might very well destroy the whole port together with some of the surrounding territory."

Einstein ended his letter by saying that Germany could be in the process of constructing the same weapon. Years later, Einstein would lament the decision to write the letter. He was a pacifist and hated war. He justified it on the fact that Hitler was advancing in his research and could make the bomb before America. He knew it could destroy the world.

The first test of an atom bomb conducted at New Mexico's Alamogordo Bombing and Gunnery
Range on 16 July 1945. Courtesy National Archives

Roosevelt took Einstein's letter seriously. He appointed a secret
commission to study the feasibility of the project. Once it was clear
that the atomic bomb could be made, FDR decided to move
forward. On October 9th, 1941, less than two months before Pearl
Harbor, the President gave the authority and responsibility to
Vannevar Bush, head of the National Defense Research Committee
to do all that was necessary to create the first nuclear device to be
used in warfare.

Franklin Roosevelt alone in the White House, 1941, Courtesy National Archives

Roosevelt made his choice only in the presence of Bush and Vice President Henry Wallace and no one else. He did not bring in other members of his Administration or the Congress. He felt that the level of secrecy was so important that the responsibility and the decision could be his and his alone. It was the largest secret project ever undertaken by the United States.

FDR told Bush to proceed aggressively and spend whatever was necessary to achieve the goal of produce the atomic bomb. By the time it was completed, 130,000 people were employed on the Manhattan Project. It cost $2 billion equivalent to nearly $30 billion today.

Franklin Roosevelt Addressing a Joint Session of Congress on December 8th, 1941 asking for a Declaration of War against Japan, Courtesy Library of Congress

Franklin Delano Roosevelt and the Attack on Pearl Harbor

On December 7th, 1941, the Japanese attached Pearl Harbor. President Franklin Roosevelt had to immediately sort out conflicting and inaccurate information to understand the details of the attack, the loss of life and the impact on Navy. More importantly, he prepared his address to the Congress to ask for a declaration of war against the Empire of Japan.

FDR in 1942 at age 60 at the start of World War II, Courtesy of Aunt Ethel's War

Franklin Roosevelt had assembled a splendid Cabinet of hard working, dedicated officials who were experts in their field. Without consulting his team, FDR decided on a short message mentioning only Japan. His senior foreign policy and military advisers wanted a long explanation to demonstrate how the United States had done everything possible to preserve peace. They wanted him to declare war on Germany and Italy as well. His Cabinet officers were unanimously opposed to Roosevelt's brief address. They discussed and argued the issue into the night.

Secretary of State Cordell Hull insisted that "the most important war in 500 years deserved more than a short statement." Secretary of War Henry Stimson added that "Germany had inspired and planned this whole affair and that the President should so state in his message." Hull pressed the President to give a detailed address that would demonstrate the history of "Japan's lawless conduct," and connect the attack on Pearl Harbor to the Nazis. Stimson agreed. [128] Franklin Roosevelt rejected their recommendations.

He trusted his instincts, which were usually correct. His goal was to speak to the American people. They would be listening to his every word on the radio. It was the people who counted. He was asking them to send their children to fight and die. The President was also concerned about giving the enemy too much information about the extent of the attack on Pearl Harbor. He did not want to ask for a declaration of war against Germany and Italy at that moment. FDR understood public opinion. Polls indicated that a conflict with Japan was more popular than one with the other Axis powers. Franklin Roosevelt was right and he had the strength to over-rule his secretaries of war, state and navy. He followed his strategic sense of what was right and wrong. At the time, there were no instant surveys or round the clock TV coverage to tell him the national mood. If he had followed the suggestions of his Cabinet, there would be no "Day of Infamy" speech, which is one of the greatest examples of Presidential oratory and leadership in American history. [129]

Yesterday, December 7th, 1941...a date which will live in infamy the United States of America was suddenly and deliberately

---

[128] Steven M. Gillon Scholar-in-Residence at History and Professor of History at the University of Oklahomahttp://www.huffingtonpost.com/steven-m-gillon/fdr-pearl-harbor_b_1115034.html

[129] Gillon

attacked by naval and air forces of the Empire of Japan... With confidence in our armed forces, with the unbounding determination of our people, we will gain the inevitable triumph -- so help us God. **Franklin Roosevelt Speech to Congress, December 8th, 1941.**

Franklin Roosevelt Signing Declaration of War against Japan, December 8th, 1941, Courtesy Library of Congress

Evacuation of the Japanese Americans from West Coast areas under U.S. Army war emergency order. 1942, Courtesy Library of Congress

The Internment of Japanese Americans

After the Japanese attack on Pearl Harbor, the US moved rapidly to prepare for the war effort militarily and domestically. Franklin Roosevelt faced the dilemma of dealing with a two front war in the Far East and Europe. He also had to deal with the fate of Japanese Americans who lived on the West Coast of the United States. There were hundreds of thousands of them. Many were second and third generation Americans. Their loyalties were challenged. "The Japanese race is an enemy race," wrote Lt. Gen. John DeWitt, the man in charge of the Western Defense Command. "And while many second- and third-generation Japanese born on United States soil, possessed of United States citizenship, have become 'Americanized,' the racial strains are undiluted." [130] Attorney General Francis Biddle and Army Deputy Chief of Staff Mark Clark were against internment of the Japanese. FDR believe he was protecting the homeland from espionage. He feared that the loyalties of Japanese Americans would lie more for Japan than the United States

---

[130] The War, Civil Rights, Japanese Americans,
http://www.pbs.org/thewar/at_home_civil_rights_japanese_american.htm

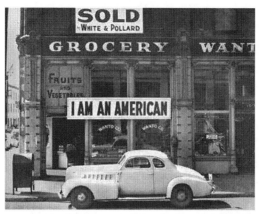

A store owner's response to anti-Japanese sentiment in the wake of the Pearl Harbor attack, Oakland, Calif., 1942. Courtesy National Archives

Nevertheless, the President signed Executive Order 9066 on February 19th, 1942. It authorized the military to remove anyone from any part of the country that they believe were a threat to national security. More than 110,000 Japanese Americans were rounded up and shipped to camps in Wyoming, Arkansas, and Arizona. Thousands of Italian and German aliens would also be interred. Millions of citizens who were from Germany or Italy would remain free to live normal lives. It was the Japanese who were singled out. "It took no great effort of imagination to see the hatred of many Americans for the enemy turned on us, who looked so much like him," observed Senator Daniel Inouye, who was 17 years old at the time. His life and that of his family was swept up in the aftermath of FDR's decision. [131] The injustice perpetrated against Japanese Americans during World War II is an example of how the government can abridge constitutional liberties in times of emergencies with terrible results.[132]

---

[131] The War, Civil Rights, Japanese Americans,
[132] Ibid The War, Civil Rights, Japanese Americans,

Twenty five years after WWII ended the US Congress set up a commission to investigate the legacy of the camps. Interviews and testimonies were gathered. The commission's final report called the incarceration a "grave injustice" motivated by "racial prejudice, war hysteria and the failure of political leadership."[133]

President Ronald Reagan signing the Civil Liberties Act of 1988, Aug. 10, 1988, Washington, D.C.
Courtesy of National Archives

Ronald Reagan, in 1988 signed the Civil Liberties Act to compensate more than 100,000 people of Japanese descent who were incarcerated in the camps. The law offered a formal apology and compensation to survivors. It was approved after a decade long fight by the Japanese-American community.[134]

---

[133] Personal Justice Denied, June, 1983 Report of the Commission on Wartime Internment of Civilians, http://www.archives.gov/research/japanese-americans/justice-denied/part-2-recommendations.pdf

[134] Personal Justice Denied

Harry Truman: Judgment at Nuremberg

"If we do not learn from history, we are doomed to repeat it."
George Santayana

We must work to bind up the wounds of a suffering world—to build an abiding peace, a peace rooted in justice and in law. We can build such a peace only by hard, toilsome, painstaking work—by understanding and working with our allies in peace as we have in war. Harry Truman

It was the afternoon of April 12th, 1945. That day, the Vice President presided over the Senate as usual. Harry Truman had replaced Vice President Henry Wallace on the ticket for 1944. The Party wanted someone strong to help win the election. They also knew that Franklin Roosevelt was dying. Wallace was considered too far to the left to take on the role of Chief Executive. Truman was a compromise candidate who had worked to pass New Deal legislation. He was considered honest and tough.

President Roosevelt, Vice President-elect Truman and Vice President Wallace, November 10, 1944, after the Democratic ticket's election victory. Courtesy National Archives

It was customary for Truman and House Speaker Sam Rayburn to have their traditional drink of bourbon and water after a long day of Senate proceedings. Suddenly, the Vice President was called to the phone. It was Steve Early, President Roosevelt's chief spokesperson. He asked him to come to the White House immediately. The Vice President expected that he would be given some important legislative mission.

In FDR's private quarters he found himself with the First Lady. "Harry, the President is dead," said Eleanor Roosevelt. Truman was shocked. "Is there anything I can do for you," he asked. "Is there anything we can do for you, Harry?" she responded. "For you are the one in trouble now."[135]

Truman said later that he felt he had "been struck by a bolt of lightning…and that the moon, the stars and the planets had all fallen on me…I felt as if I had lived five lifetimes in those first days as President." Truman had been Vice President 82 days. He met Roosevelt twice during that time yet remained uninformed about the major events concerning the war and the Administration's post war plans. Harry Truman was frightened.

He was no Franklin Roosevelt. He was not charismatic and had a fragile ego, which few observers could perceive. Unlike, FDR, he did not have a political streak and would not manipulate others to gain leverage. Truman was direct and considered himself a straight shooter who made decisions based on facts. He realized that the best way to gain trust with the people was to move forward aggressively to fulfill FDR's wartime and post wartime programs. The new commander in chief needed to show vigor and activism and he did.

Truman asked Roosevelt's Cabinet to remain in place. He said he would take their advice but would be the one making the decisions which he expected them to support. The new President immediately set out to make difficult choices to deal with ending the war and reconstruction of Europe and Japan. The New York Times described it this way:

"In war-ravaged Europe in those years, Truman and the United States established peace and held back Soviet expansion and built economic and political stability through the Truman Doctrine, the Marshall Plan and the North Atlantic Treaty Organization. In the

---

[135] Eleanor and Harry: The Correspondence of Eleanor Roosevelt and Harry S. Truman". *Harry S. Truman Library & Museum*. Retrieved July 28, 2012.

Mideast he recognized the State of Israel. In the Far East the President imposed peace and constitutional democracy on the Japanese enemy, tried valiantly to save China from Communism and chose to wage war in Korea to halt aggression. In the United States, Truman led the nation's conversion from war to peace, while maintaining a stable and prosperous economy."[136]

One of the most critical decisions facing Truman was the trial of Nazi's accused of war crimes. In 1943, Roosevelt, Stalin and Churchill met in Tehran. Stalin wanted summary executions of German officers. Churchill disagreed and called for trials of those involved in crimes against humanity. Secretary of War Henry Stimson was charged with coming up with a plan for trying the Nazi's at the end of the War. It was entitled *"Trial of European War Criminals"* As the War progressed toward a conclusion, the Allies were unable to come to grips with whether or not to hold the trials at all or conduct summary executions.

---

[136] Alden Whitman, Harry S. Truman: Decisive President, New York Times, December 27th, 1972, http://www.nytimes.com/learning/general/onthisday/bday/0508.html

British Troops burning the last building at the Belsen Concentration Camp, May 21st, 1945, Courtesy British Official Photo

The proposal to proceed or not was presented to President Truman. The Chief Justice of the Supreme Court, Harlan Fiske Stone and Justice William O. Douglas were opposed to the trials. Stone accused the Chief Prosecutor of conducting "a high grade lynching party." [137] Truman was not swayed by opposition to the trials. Jeffrey Lawrence, the chief British Judge at the Nuremberg Tribunal summed up the situation:

"There were, I suppose, three possible courses: to let the atrocities which had been committed go unpunished; to put the perpetrators to death or punish them by executive action; or to try them. Which

---

[137] Dönitz at Nuremberg: A Reappraisal', H. K. Thompson, Jr. and Henry Strutz, (Torrance, Calif.: 1983)

was it to be? Was it possible to let such atrocities go unpunished? Could France, could Russia, could Holland, Belgium, Norway, Czechoslovakia, Poland or Yugoslavia be expected to consent to such a course? ... It will be remembered that after the First World War alleged criminals were handed over to be tried by Germany, and what a farce that was! The majority got off and such sentences as were inflicted were derisory and were soon remitted."[138]

On May 2nd, 1945, the President appointed Robert H. Jackson, Associate Justice of the Supreme Court of the United States to lead the prosecution of the chief Nazi war lords at the Nuremberg Tribunal. Truman gave Jackson free rein to choose his team and represent the United States at the trial. Jackson worked to achieve a consensus among the Allies which was called the London Charter. It became the basis for the proceedings before the International Military Tribunal. It lasted ten months. Among the twenty-two defendants were Hermann Goering, President of the Reichstag, and Albert Speer, Minister of Armaments and War Production.

---

[138] Lawrence 1947, pp. 152–3. This speech by Lawrence is reprinted in Mettraux 2008, pp. 290–9.

The defendants at Nuremberg. Courtesy of the National Archives.

The trial opened on November 19th, 1945. The indictments against 24 major war criminals and seven organizations, which included the Nazi Party, the Reich Court and the General Staff and High Command of Germany, were for: [139]

1. Participation in a common plan or conspiracy for the accomplishment of a crime against peace
2. Planning, initiating and waging wars of aggression and other crimes against peace
3. War crimes

[139] Henkel (ed.), Matthias (2011), Memoriam Nuernberger Prozesse, exhibition catalogue (German), Nuremberg: Museen der Stadt Nuernberg, 78 pp.

4. Crimes against humanity

"It was the first time an international tribunal had sought to sentence the leaders of a regime - politicians, army officers and economic advisors - even though in some cases direct responsibility for specific criminal acts could not be attributed to them.

As a group, they were seen as initiators, aides, organizers and executers of crimes against humanity. They were accused of orchestrating wars of aggression, murdering civilians and prisoners of war, deporting people, plundering, engaging in racial persecution, murdering European Jews and occupying numerous European countries."[140]

On October 1st, 1946 the verdict was rendered. Three of the defendants were acquitted, four sentenced to prison terms from 10 to 20 years, three sentenced to life imprisonment and twelve were sentenced to death by hanging. Ten of the condemned Nazi criminals were executed two weeks later. Goering escaped his fate by taking a cyanide capsule hours before his execution.

The American authorities conducted subsequent Nuremberg Trials in their occupied zone. Other trials conducted after the Nuremberg Trials include the following:[141]

- Auschwitz Trial
- Belsen Trial
- Belzec Trial before the 1st Munich District Court in the mid-1960s, of eight SS-men of the Belzec extermination camp

---

[140] Nuremberg Trials Left a Lasting Legacy. http://www.dw.com/en/nuremberg-trials-left-a-lasting-legacy/a-6237501
[141] Kevin Jon Heller (2011). The Trials. Introduction: the indictments, biographical information, and the verdicts. The Nuremberg Military Tribunals and the Origins of International Criminal Law (Oxford University Press). pp. 85–. Retrieved 10 January 2015

- Chełmno trials of the Chełmno extermination camp personnel, held in Poland and in Germany. The cases were decided almost twenty years apart
- Dachau Trials
- Frankfurt Auschwitz Trials
- Majdanek trials, the longest Nazi war crimes trial in history, spanning over 30 years
- Mauthausen-Gusen camp trials
- Ravensbrück Trial
- Sobibor trial held in Hagen, Germany in 1965 against the SS-men of the Sobibor extermination camp
- Treblinka trials in Düsseldorf, Germany

The legacy of the Nuremberg Trials led do the adoption by the United Nations affirming "the principles in international law recognized by the Charter of the Nuremberg Tribunal and by the judgement of the Tribunal." In 1950 the International Law Commission submitted seven principles to the UN as the basis of a code of crimes against humanity that are still in effect today.

As he announced the end of the War in Europe, President Truman expressed his feelings that coincided with his decision about Nuremberg:

Our rejoicing is sobered and subdued by a supreme consciousness of the terrible price we have paid to rid the world of Hitler and his evil band. Let us not forget, my fellow Americans, the sorrow and the heartache which today abide in the homes of so many of our neighbors—neighbors whose most priceless possession has been rendered as a sacrifice to redeem our liberty.

2016 Selecting the President

During the commemoration of the seventieth anniversary of the liberation of Auschwitz, A member of the Canadian Parliament, Irwin Cotler, said these words:[142]

"Finally, we must remember – and celebrate – the survivors of the Holocaust, the true heroes of humanity. For they witnessed and endured the worst of inhumanity, but somehow found, in the depths of their own humanity, the courage to go on, to rebuild their lives as they helped build our communities.

And so, together with them we must remember and pledge – not as an idle slogan but as an injunction to act –– that never again will we be indifferent to incitement and hate, never again will we be silent in the face of evil, never again will we indulge racism and anti-Semitism, never again will we ignore the plight of the vulnerable, and never again will we be indifferent in the face of mass atrocity and impunity.

We will speak up and act against racism, against hate, against anti-Semitism, against mass atrocity, against injustice, and against the crime of crimes whose name we should shudder to mention: genocide."

---

[142] Irwin Cotler, 70 years later: Universal lessons for our time, The Jerusalem Post, January 29th, 2015. http://www.jpost.com/Opinion/70-years-later-Universal-lessons-for-our-time-389450

The Decision to Drop the Atomic Bomb

Atomic bombs over Hiroshima and Nagasaki, August, 1945, Courtesy National Archives

Harry Truman, Courtesy National Archives

Franklin Delano Roosevelt died on April 12th, 1945. Harry Truman was sworn in the same day. He had been Vice President for eighty days. He had met with FDR twice since inauguration day on January 20th. He knew that a weapon capable of mass destruction had been developed and that it could bring an end to the war with Japan. When President Truman learned of the Manhattan Project he realized he faced a decision that no President of the United States had ever encountered. Ending the war with Japan was in his grasp.

Raising the flag at Iwo Jima, Courtesy National Archives

It could save the lives of hundreds of thousands of American soldiers and sailors who would be forced to invade Japan to compel the Japanese to surrender. At the same time, it would unleash the most terrible weapon ever conceived.

Americans were exhausted from four years of war in Europe and the Pacific. Over 150,000 Japanese and Allied personnel died in the battle of Okinawa. It was the bloodiest battle of the Pacific war and had a profound influence on President Truman and his decision to use the atomic bomb to bring about the surrender of Japan.

Japanese cities were being fire bombed. Despite the relentless destruction, the Japanese military refused to give up. An army of two million soldiers were prepared to defend the Japanese homeland. Truman had to decide to either use the bomb or conduct one of the longest and bloodiest invasions in history. He consulted with officers, scientists and diplomats to determine the best course of action.

The US military estimated that an amphibious landing could result in a million Allied casualties. The President had to weigh the cost in American lives as well as Japanese lives. He felt that using the bomb would end the war and save lives on both sides. Continuing the war was not an option. Over 3,500 Japanese kamikaze raids had produced extensive loss of American military personnel and great destruction.

Truman rejected the idea of a demonstration bomb to shake the Japanese military into submission. There was no certainty that they would capitulate even if the test succeeded. A failed test would be make matters worse than no test at all. Truman believed that the new weapon would act like the massive fire-bombing of Tokyo or Dresden. The scientific community did not foresee the immense effects of radiation poisoning. The President decided to use the first nuclear weapon to bring an end to the bloodshed.

The plane that dropped the first atomic bombs, The Enola Gay, August, 1945, Courtesy National
Archives

On August 6th, 1945, the first atomic blast occurred over the city of
Hiroshima.   Within minutes, 70,000 Japanese citizens were
vaporized. Another 100,000 died in the months and years to come
from radiation sickness. The Japanese refused to lay down their
arms. A second nuclear device was unleashed three days later on
Nagasaki. 80,000 people died instantly. [143] The nuclear age was
born along with the possibility of atomic war.

*The atomic bomb made the prospect of future war unendurable. It
has led us up those last few steps to the mountain pass; and beyond
there is a different country.* **J. Robert Oppenheimer**

*As human beings, our greatness lies not so much in being able to
remake the world - that is the myth of the atomic age - as in being
able to remake ourselves.* **Mahatma Gandhi**

---

[143] Us history.org The Decision to Drop the Atom Bomb, http://www.ushistory.org/us/51g.asp

The Firing of General Douglas MacArthur

General Douglas MacArthur, in the Philippines 1944, Courtesy National Archives

Douglas MacArthur was one of the most celebrated and popular Generals in American history. He was former Superintendent of the US Military Academy at West Point; among the youngest major generals in Army history; Military Advisor to the Commonwealth Government of the Philippines, Commander of the US Army forces in the Far East; Supreme Commander of the Southwestern Pacific forces; presided over the Japanese surrender in World War II;

oversaw the occupation of Japan and received the Congressional Medal of Honor. War broke out in Korea in 1950 when North Korea invaded the South. MacArthur was called back to head up United Nations forces. At the beginning of the conflict, MacArthur had prepared some brilliant strategies that saved the South from falling into the hands of communist forces from the North. MacArthur pushed for a policy to invade the North.

Truman and MacArthur meeting in South Korea, Courtesy National Archives

President Truman accepted the plan but was concerned that Communist China could enter the conflict. MacArthur met with Truman in October, 1950 and assured him that the chances of China entering the war were slim. A month later, hundreds of thousands of Chinese soldiers hurled themselves again American forces driving them back into the South. MacArthur asked permission to bomb China. Truman refused. He did not want to expand the conflict. His goal was to limit the communist advance and save South Korea from being taken over by the North.

The Outcome of the Firing of General MacArthur, Courtesy National Archives

MacArthur disagreed publically with the President. He made a series of statements that bordered on insubordination. President Truman had to assert the authority of his office and civilian authority over the military. Truman's standing in the polls and his popularity with the public was one of the lowest for any President. This had no effect on his decision. Truman listened to his Secretary of Defense, George Marshall, and his Secretary of State, Dean Acheson. They told the President that firing MacArthur would provoke a firestorm in the press and with the public. He listened to his team but kept his own counsel. Truman knew the political consequences of his decision. He knew it would hurt him and his Party in the elections of 1952. Even so, he knew what the proper choice to make was. On April 11th, 1951, General Douglas

MacArthur, hero of World War II and one of the most popular military figures in American history, was relieved of his command.

Paul Loring, 1951 Courtesy The Providence Evening Bulletin

He returned to the United States to a welcome befitting a great hero. A ticker tape parade in New York and parades and ceremonies elsewhere marked the end of a magnificent career. MacArthur addressed a joint session of Congress. His farewell address received fifty standing ovations. He defended his actions in Korea and his disagreement with the President. He ended his speech with these words:[144]

I am closing my 52 years of military service. When I joined the Army, even before the turn of the century, it was the fulfillment of all of my boyish hopes and dreams. The world has turned over many times since I took the oath on the plain at West Point, and the hopes and dreams have long since vanished, but I still remember the refrain of one of the most popular barrack ballads of that day which proclaimed most proudly that "old soldiers never die; they just fade away."

And like the old soldier of that ballad, I now close my military career and just fade away, an old soldier who tried to do his duty as God gave him the light to see that duty. Good Bye.

---

[144] Torricelli, Robert G.; Carroll, Andrew; Goodwin, Doris Kearns (2008). In Our Own Words Extraordinary Speeches of the American Century. Washington Square Press. ISBN 978-0-7434-1052-6. OCLC 45144217. Pp-185-188

MacArthur speaking at Soldier Field in Chicago in 1951, Courtesy National Archives

There will be moments in the next four years when the President we elect in 2016 will have to make crucial decisions. The legacy of the decisions of FDR and Truman, for example, are still with us today. We must remember that the Commander in Chief we select in 2016 will make choices that will affect our children and grandchildren and their children.

One's philosophy is not best expressed in words; it is expressed in the choices one makes... and the choices we make are ultimately our responsibility. **Eleanor Roosevelt**

Every person has free choice. Free to obey or disobey the Natural Laws. Your choice determines the consequences. Nobody ever did, or ever will, escape the consequences of his choices.
Alfred A. Montapert

It is our choices... that show what we truly are, far more than our abilities. **J. K. Rowling**

We must make the choices that enable us to fulfill the deepest capacities of our real selves. **Thomas Merton**

You are doomed to make choices. This is life's greatest paradox.

Wayne Dyer

There are two primary choices in life: to accept conditions as they exist, or accept the responsibility for changing them.

Denis Waitley

Chapter Ten: Humility

It was pride that changed angels into devils; it is humility that makes men as angels. **Saint Augustine**

We come nearest to the great when we are great in humility. **R. Ta**

Pride makes us artificial... humility makes us real. **Thomas Merton**

The principles of living greatly include the capacity to face trouble with courage, disappointment with cheerfulness, and trial with humility. **Thomas S. Mons**

Humility is the true key to success. Successful people lose their way at times. They often embrace and overindulge from the fruits of success. Humility halts this arrogance and self-indulging trap. Humble people share the credit and wealth, remaining focused and hungry to continue the journey of success. **Rick Pitino**

A grateful heart is a beginning of greatness. It is an expression of humility. It is a foundation for the development of such virtues as prayer, faith, courage, contentment, happiness, love, and well-being. **James E. Faust**

There is no respect for others without humility in one's self. **Henri Frederic Amiel**

The first test of a truly great man is his humility. By humility I don't mean doubt of his powers or hesitation in speaking his opinion, but merely an understanding of the relationship of what he can say and what he can do. **John Ruskin**

A President without humility will not survive. The Office requires a humble occupant who is willing to learn and admit what they do not know. Humility allows them to listen. It gives them the temperament to admit mistakes without appearing weak. It demands that they consult with experts and pick leaders of their team who may be perceived has being superior but can get the job done. A President who builds a strong "Brain Trust" of the best and the brightest will need to deal with extraordinary individuals who are professionals and will know more than they do. Humility to listen and learn matched with self-confidence that is not arrogance is the key formula to tackling great challenges. It allows dissenters and advocates to have their say without worrying about the consequences. They know that the President is searching for facts, solutions and will tolerate disagreements as long as they stress problems and not personalities. The President that stands out above all others for having been both humble and immensely successful was Abraham Lincoln.

Abraham Lincoln, Courtesy Library of Congress

The Humility of Abraham Lincoln

The humility of Abe Lincoln that he carried into the White House came from his modest beginnings and the enormous sense of empathy he had for others and for the world around him and for being unconventional for his times. He grew up on the prairie where men were measured by their ability to hunt, farm, drink and smoke and how harshly they treated women. Lincoln was a teetotaler; he loved animals and was almost a vegetarian. He did not smoke, drink or chew tobacco. In 1836 he advocated for women's right to vote. Abraham Lincoln was by no means politically correct for his times. Yet within his difference was a sense of self-worth and respect for all creation and all human beings.

Lincoln was a man who had more failures than successes in life. It was those setbacks that contributed to his humility and his ability to understand that each person is fighting their own battle for survival. He was rejected twice by women he loved. His marriage to Mary Todd was not an easy one. They had four sons. Edward died when he was four. Willie died at twelve and Tad at eighteen. The loss of their children was impossible to forget for Mary and Abraham. He suffered from sadness and, some claim, clinical depression for most of his life.

He was not a success in business. He failed at his first bid for elected office. Later he served four terms in the Illinois legislature. He was elected to the House of Representatives in 1846. He supported Zachary Taylor for President. Lincoln hoped to be appointed Commissioner of the General Land Office. The job went to rival. He went back to practicing law. He lost his Senate bid to Stephen Douglas in 1858. Despite professional setbacks and personal heartbreaks, he never gave up. Two years after losing the race for the Senate he was elected President. He was not his Party's first choice. There were other candidates who had more experience in Washington politics like New York Governor William H. Seward, Congressman Edward Bates and well known attorney Salmon P. Chase. Lincoln was being positioned as a second choice if the leading candidates fell. Against these distinguished leaders, a nearly unknown "prairie lawyer" and one-term Congressman was chosen as the Presidential candidate of the Republican Party in 1860. After the election, Lincoln would select these men, his "team of rivals" to help him govern. Edwin Stanton, a man he knew as a lawyer, was chosen to be Secretary of War. Lincoln met him when they pleaded a case together. Stanton did not like him and Lincoln knew this. He even said derogatory things about him. This did not faze Lincoln. He saw in Stanton the toughness, integrity and determination needed to harness the military might of the nation to fight the Civil War.

A cartoon in 1864, took a swing at Lincoln's Administration featuring Lincoln, William Fessenden, Edwin Stanton, William Seward and Gideon Welles

In the beginning, the choice of Stanton appeared a mistake. He continued his condescending ways. At times it seemed that the Secretary of War was working at cross purposes of the President. Stanton disobeyed Lincoln when he felt he was wrong. Stanton's attitude did not affect Lincoln. He forcefully corrected him to set the record straight and make sure his decisions were followed. He rarely took offense, even at the gravest insults. Lincoln focused on the big picture—winning the war. If his Cabinet liked him was of little concern to Abraham Lincoln. His preoccupation was their doing their job well and preserving the Union which was his vision and his goal.

One day, a congressman arrived at Lincoln's office, reporting that the secretary of war had not only countermanded a direct order from Lincoln but also called the president a damned fool for issuing it. "Did Stanton say I was a damned fool?" asked Lincoln. "He did sir, and repeated it," replied the congressman.

This accusation was no small thing. If true, it meant that a prominent cabinet member—the secretary of war, no less—had just ignored his commander in chief's direct order and then compounded his offense by insulting the president of the United States in the presence of a sitting congressman. By any military standard, Secretary Stanton was guilty of out-and-out mutiny. Lincoln's response reveals volumes about the man's character:

"If Stanton said I was a damned fool, then I must be one, for he is nearly always right, and generally says what he means. I will step over and see him."[145]

Personal feelings were subsumed to vital interests of the nation. This was humility and leadership at its best.

In 1838, Lincoln gave one of his first public addresses. It was to the Young Men's Lyceum of Springfield, Illinois. Lincoln was 28 years old. He had just moved to the town from a pioneer village. The incident that provoked the speech was the murder of a young black man in St. Louis, Missouri. He was burned to death by a mob. Lincoln spoke about the dangers of slavery and how it could corrupt

[145] *Donovan Campbell, The Leader's Code, http://theleaderscode.com/excerpts/humility/*

the government and body politic. He told the story and what it meant:[146]

A mulatto man, by the name of McIntosh, was seized in the street, dragged to the suburbs of the city, chained to a tree, and actually burned to death; and all within a single hour from the time he had been a freeman, attending to his own business, and at peace with the world. Such are the effects of mob law...

Mob rule would mean mob justice, in Lincoln's view. The guilty and the innocent would be swept up in rage and irrationality. Even the members of multitude that took justice in their own hands would not be spared. They too would be victims of the horde that tramples the law. Lincoln was preaching for human rights and respect for the Bill of Rights, the Constitution and the Declaration of Independence. Twenty-two years later, Lincoln would defend his fight to preserve the Union and end slavery referring back to basic principles of the American republic embodied in its sacred documents and history.

In the Lyceum speech, Lincoln revealed his sense of humility. He said every nation created "Napoleons" who had "towering ambition" and had a thirst to be famous. At the inception of the United States, one could be renown by working to strengthen the young nation's institutions. Now those were in place, in Lincoln's view. "But now, success is assured. We are a success. And you don't get eternal fame by assuring the success of something that's already successful. You get it by changing the world." Abraham Lincoln was ready to lead. He was not interested in glory. He wanted to right wrongs. He was humble but strong. He carried these qualities into the White House.

Lincoln liked people. He had a way where he could make the farmer, the artisan and the banker feel at home. Most of his political enemies avoided meeting him. Once someone was in his presence they felt a natural liking for Lincoln. It was a trait that he used to

---

[146] Collected Works of Abraham Lincoln, edited by Roy P. Basler et al.
http://www.abrahamlincolnonline.org/lincoln/speeches/lyceum.htm

win over the opposition and to convince his Cabinet to his point of view.

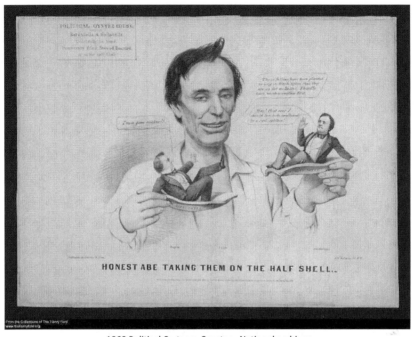

1860 Political Cartoon, Courtesy National archives

Lincoln was self-deprecating and modest even about his responsibilities. He spoke about being "a humble instrument in the hands of the Almighty."[147] Lincoln managed to hold his temper even under the most stressful conditions. He responded to complaints, often times in writing. He was straight forward but sensitive in his responses. Your words of kindness are very grateful,

---

[147] Michael Burlingame, editor, *Lincoln Observed: Civil War Dispatches of Noah Brooks*, p. 208 (from Noah Brooks, "Personal Recollections of Abraham Lincoln, *Harper's Monthly Magazine*, May 1865). http://abrahamlincolnsclassroom.org/abraham-lincoln-in-depth/abraham-lincolns-personality/

but your suspicions that I intend you an injustice are very painful to me. I assure you such suspicions are groundless."[148]

Lincoln with his son Tad, Courtesy the Library of Congress

Lincoln concentrated on others' point of view. He worked to repair hurt feelings especially when it could escalate in permanent resentment. Lincoln gave credit easily and took responsibility when things went badly. He credited Grant with defeating the South, for example, but admitted his errors even when the failure was that of subordinate. Lincoln was never provoked by petty situations. He was not jealous or held grudges.

Lincoln transformed his humility and human kindness into leadership strength. He combined it with self-confidence and sincere altruism. It became an essential quality of his mystique and

---

[148] Ibid. Burlingame

the secret to his success. Lincoln showed that it takes greater effort and valor to be humble than to be egocentric.

Humble leaders are able to genuinely relate to and empathize with ordinary people. They don't consider themselves better or more important than others, and are able to easily acknowledge their own shortcomings and laugh at their blunders. Humble leaders realize they don't have all the answers and they are willing to heed the advice and learn from the feedback of others.[149]

At its essence, humility is nothing more than a realistic and unflinching view of yourself and your relationships. Humility is not self-deceit, self-denial, or self-flagellation. A leader grounds humility in an honest assessment of strengths and weaknesses, an inventory of the good, the bad, and the ugly. This self-understanding and self-reflection constitutes humility. By gaining a deeper and more realistic knowledge of ourselves, we become more humble. **Donovan Campbell**

Humility may be the most difficult quality we will discover in the candidates for President in 2016, yet it is among the most essential. At times it is mistaken for weakness. The gentle toughness of Lincoln combined with his ability to not take himself seriously made him a better and stronger leader who could know himself as well as know others. A humble President will know what they do not know and to compensate for it by taking action to find the best people to help him or her govern in 2016.

---

[149] Dan Nielsen, Presidential Leadership: Learning from United States Presidential Libraries & Museums (Dan Nielsen Company, 2013), p. 272.

Lincoln Memorial, Courtesy National Archives

Chapter Eleven: Passionate and Energetic

Every great dream begins with a dreamer. Always remember, you have within you the strength, the patience, and the passion to reach for the stars to change the world. **Harriet Tubman**

Great ambition is the passion of a great character. Those endowed with it may perform very good or very bad acts. All depends on the principles which direct them. **Napoleon Bonaparte**

Passion is energy. Feel the power that comes from focusing on what excites you. **Oprah Winfrey**

We can each define ambition and progress for ourselves. The goal is to work toward a world where expectations are not set by the stereotypes that hold us back, but by our personal passion, talents and interests. **Sheryl Sandberg**

Passion is one great force that unleashes creativity, because if you're passionate about something, then you're more willing to take risks. **Yo-Yo Ma**

Leadership is not about a title or a designation. It's about impact, influence and inspiration. Impact involves getting results, influence is about spreading the passion you have for your work, and you have to inspire team-mates and customers.
Robin S. Sharma

Success comes to those who dedicate everything to their passion in life. To be successful, it is also very important to be humble and never let fame or money travel to your head. **A. R. Rahman**

Presidents Must Lead with Passion and Vigor

Our most successful and memorable Presidents led with passion and vigor. It was the love of the job, the desire to exercise the power and manage the levers of the Presidency and the desire to achieve that made the difference. Within passion is energy. Our most energetic leaders took on the duties with gusto. This love of life, this hunger to accomplish, and this high level of vitality concentrated on success is innate and not created. Few can learn to be "passionate" about the Presidency. "The first thing that has to be recognized is that one cannot train someone to be passionate--it's either in their DNA or it's not," says Richard Branson, CEO of Virgin Airlines. "Believe me, I have tried and failed on more than one occasion and it cannot be done so don't waste your time and energy trying to light a fire under flame-resistant people."[150]

What distinguishes one passionate and energetic President from another is their approach to the Presidency, their character and how much they enjoy the job. How active they are is a clear sign. Active Presidents often perform better. They lead with fervor and dynamism. How briskly they approach problems and how much drive they devote to the task defines them as active vs. passive Presidents. Close attention needs to be given to these qualities during campaigns to avoid putting into office the wrong person at the wrong time.

---

[150] Richard Branson, The Virgin Way, Part Three, The Fruits of Passion, Penguin, New York, 2014, http://www.inc.com/richard-branson/passion-is-innate.html

James David Barber devoted considerable attention to predicting performance in the White House. [151] Barber believed that the Presidency was much more than an institution. It was a set of popular feelings that were embodied in the Presidency. The Congress and the bureaucracy are often viewed as distinct and complex organizations by the public. The Presidency is where the people make sense of issues and where they rest their hopes and fears. It is the closest we get to an American monarchy.

Presidential Styles

The founding fathers left many things vague about the Presidency. They knew that each new entrant would define the powers differently and distinctly. As a result, the Office has evolved and changed based on the style and character of each occupant. Barber classified Presidents in four categories grounded on the activity or passivity that they brought to the position.

Active/Negative:

They are gamblers who take risks. They do not like the political give and take and, as a result, rarely see the drawbacks of their decisions. Woodrow Wilson, Herbert Hoover, Lyndon Johnson, Richard Nixon and George W. Bush fall into this category.

Active/Positive:

They love the position. They pursue the duties aggressively. They strive for achievement and success. Abraham Lincoln, Franklin Roosevelt, Theodore Roosevelt, Harry Truman, John Kennedy,

---

[151] "Presidential Character and How to Foresee It," chapter 1 of The Presidential Character: Predicting Performance in the White House, 4th ed. by James David Barber, pp. 1-1 1, 493. Prentice Hall, New York, 1992.

Jimmy Carter and recent observers have included Bill Clinton and Barack Obama.

Passive/Positive:

These are Presidents who are often loved but usually have few accomplishments. They search for affection as their reward and are cooperative and agreeable rather than being assertive. Often times, they project an image of optimism to dispel doubts and lift spirits to reduce the pain of politics. Presidents James Madison, William Howard Taft, Warren G. Harding and Ronald Reagan were in this group according to Barber.

Passive Negative:

These are the reluctant politicians who are in the field because they feel they need to be. They do not relish the responsibilities of the Presidency but take them on as a duty to the nation. They are rarely innovators and work to keep stability. They are more laid back. George Washington is the classic case. He had to be persuaded to take on a second term. Calvin Coolidge and Dwight Eisenhower are other examples.

Candidates and Presidents do not fall neatly into these groups. It is the tendency toward certain characteristics that need to be looked at. The key is to analyze the individual's personality before they get into the White House. By so doing, we can often predict, within limits, what they will be like in Oval Office. An example is Theodore Roosevelt.

Colonel Theodore Roosevelt, Courtesy National Archives

Theodore Roosevelt: The First Modern President

Teddy Roosevelt was our first modern President. The Presidency as we know it today, with its stature and influence started with him. Edmund Morris described him this way: [152]

"They don't hold White House lunches the way they used to at the beginning of the century. On Jan. 1, 1907, for example, the guest list was as follows: a Nobel prizewinner, a physical culturalism, a naval historian, a biographer, an essayist, a paleontologist, a

---

[152] Edmund Morris, Theodore Roosevelt, Time Magazine Monday, Apr. 13, 1998

taxidermist, an ornithologist, a field naturalist, a conservationist, a big-game hunter, an editor, a critic, a ranchman, an orator, a country squire, a civil service reformer, a socialite, a patron of the arts, a colonel of the cavalry, a former Governor of New York, the ranking expert on big-game mammals in North America and the President of the U.S.

All these men were named Theodore Roosevelt."

He was truly an American phenomenon. His passion, energy and vision were unique. No President before or after him had the same qualities. He read one to three books a day. During his Presidency he wrote 150,000 letters. Henry Adams said of the President: "Power when wielded by abnormal energy is the most serious of facts...Roosevelt, more than any other man living within the range of notoriety, showed the singular primitive quality that belongs to ultimate matter--he was pure Act."[153]

In the late 19th century, political parties and the Congress dominated the political scene. Through the force of his personality and aggressive executive action, Roosevelt changed the center of American politics to the Office of the President. He believed that the President should use all powers provided by the Constitution that were not specifically denied. He fought the notion of limited government action to right wrongs and correct social imbalances. He felt the President had a special relationship and responsibility to the people. Government was an agent of progress, reform, regulation and conservation and had the duty to make society fairer and more equitable and share economic opportunities for all. He created five national parks, eighteen national monuments and countless millions of national forest preserved for generations.

Before Roosevelt, big business was given a free hand to achieve their objectives. Teddy believed that it had to be regulated and controlled in the public interest. He set out to break the large

---

[153] Ibid Morris

"trusts" and monopolies that dominated sectors of American business to make them more competitive. He changed America's posture in global affairs. Roosevelt believed the United States a global duty to protect its interests around the world.

Great White Fleet Returning to Hampton Roads, December, 1907 Courtesy Library of Congress

He vigorously pressed Congress to expand the Navy and launched the "Great White Fleet" to circle the earth and demonstrate American naval strength. The President wanted to exhibit expanding US military power and oceanic naval capability. He wanted the fleet to also enforce treaties and protect sea lanes. From a fleet of 90 small ships, many of them of wood, the fleet grew into a modern fighting force. The fleet of sixteen battleships, divided into two squadrons and various escorts, completed a circumnavigation of the globe from December 16th, 1907 to February 22, 1909.

Welcoming the Great White Fleet to Australia, 1908, Courtesy National Archives

The fleet was received in ports across the globe as an example of American strength and American friendship.

President Theodore Roosevelt (on the 12-inch (30 cm) gun turret at right) addresses officers and crewmen on *Connecticut*, in Hampton Roads, Virginia, upon her return from the Fleet's cruise around the world, 22 February 1909, Courtesy the Library of Congress

Roosevelt was determined to build the Panama Canal. He vigorously became involved in Latin American politics to do so. He ordered the building to start in 1903 after what he described as "three centuries of conversation." Teddy negotiated international peace treaties and worked to achieve a balance of power around the world.

1902 Political Cartoon of Teddy and the Trusts, Courtesy National Archives

Theodore Roosevelt introduced charisma to Presidential politics. His strong rapport with the people and his way of working closely with the media helped shape public opinion. He continued his dynamic approach to policy issues even after he left office. In 1912, The Progressive Party's New Nationalism platform echoed the liberal movements of the 1930's and 1960's that became the spirit of the New Deal, Harry Truman's Fair Deal, the New Frontier of John Kennedy and the Great Society of Lyndon Johnson.

The Presidency demands energy, good health and resiliency. Theodore Roosevelt had it. It gave him the drive to approach the

Office with passion and dedication. Can we find another Teddy in 2016?

Passion is energy. Feel the power that comes from focusing on what excites you. **Oprah Winfrey**

Enthusiasm is the yeast that makes your hopes shine to the stars. Enthusiasm is the sparkle in your eyes, the swing in your gait. The grip of your hand, the irresistible surge of will and energy to execute your ideas. **Henry Ford**

Success is almost totally dependent upon drive and persistence. The extra energy required to make another effort or try another approach is the secret of winning. **Denis Waitley**

The energy of the mind is the essence of life. **Aristotle**

Chapter Twelve: Flexible and Comfortable with Change

Great leaders are almost always great simplifiers, who can cut through argument, debate, and doubt to offer a solution everybody can understand. **General Colin Powell**

Defenders of the status quo will argue that this system has served us well over the centuries, that our parliamentary traditions have combined stability and flexibility and that we should not cast away in a minute what has taken generations to build. **Ferdinand Mount**

Take advantage of the ambiguity in the world. Look at something and think what else it might be. **Roger von Oech**

On the road from the City of Skepticism, I had to pass through the Valley of Ambiguity. **Adam Smith**

It may be enough to study history in all its nuance and ambiguity for its own sake. But there is no country free of the need to find new ways of reading the past as an inspiring way of thinking about everything else, including the present. **Colm Toibin**

The battlefield is a scene of constant chaos. The winner will be the one who controls that chaos, both his own and the enemies.

Napoleon Bonaparte

From Washington to Obama, each President has dealt with change. Each era has its ambiguities and each administration has had to develop strategies to be flexible and cope with changing events. Washington had the luxury of time since information and transportation was slow compared to today. He and Lincoln, for example, were handicapped by the quality of data available and the speed at which they could receive and respond. Today information is not only abundant; it can be checked and double checked immediately for accuracy. Responses can be given instantaneously.

Twenty-first century leaders live in an era of change that appears to happen at lightning speed. The President must be resilient in the face of the unexpected. They must set the example to: [154]

Demonstrate their ability to deal with stress and pressure.

Bounce back from setbacks and disappointments.

Maintain optimism and a positive attitude in the face of new challenges and problems becoming ever more complex.

Exhibit the skill to maintain strong leadership even in the face of uncertainty.

In addition to the personal qualities they bring to the job, they will need to organize their team to handle the rapid evolution of events and challenges that will face them on a daily basis. One example was Dwight Eisenhower.

---

[154] Melanie Allen, Dealing with Ambiguity and Developing Resilience, http://www.melanieallen.co.uk/articles/dealing-with-ambiguity/?utm_campaign=LinkedIn150&utm_content=Dealing%20with%20Ambiguity%20the%20New%20Business%20Imperative

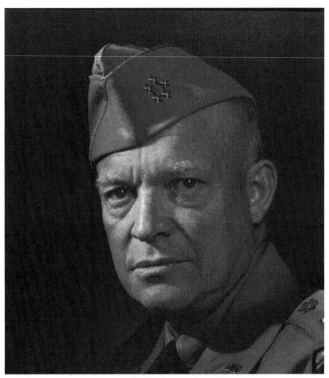

General Dwight Eisenhower, Supreme Allied Commander, 1945, Courtesy Library of Congress

Eisenhower and the National Security Council

Eisenhower was inaugurated President in 1952. His predecessors, Harry Truman and Franklin Roosevelt organized their White House in different ways. FDR often used his Brain Trust vs his Cabinet to make decisions. Truman relied on the Cabinet and his trusted experts and advisers to deal with evolving difficulties of ending the War and dealing with the aftermath. The Soviets had the atomic bomb. They had occupied Eastern Europe and installed communist regimes. The Cold War had begun. The War in Korea needed to be ended. The post-World War II occupation required conclusion. The Marshall Plan for reconstruction of Europe was nearing completion. Domestic policies needed attention like boosting employment and starting major infrastructure projects. Eisenhower was determined to simultaneously balance the budget and promote an era of peace and prosperity.

Eisenhower realized that the Cold War would be a long drawn out effort to contain communism in the world and prevent the Soviet Union from expanding its imperialistic tendencies. He felt that military means were not the answer. Eisenhower had met and dealt with many Russian leaders during the War. He believed their main goal was survival in office and not world domination, even though they preached the spread of Marxism worldwide. He felt that the Soviet empire would evaporate by decay and its inability to deal with internal problems. The essential defense for the US and its allies was fortification of democracy and prosperity. Containment of the Soviet Union demanded strengthening NATO and aid to developing countries to attain stability and reduce poverty.

Cold War Political Cartoon, Courtesy National Archives

He was concerned with the strategic and financial aspects of husbanding his resources to deal with the global Soviet threat. "No president after Eisenhower would have this appreciation of the financial aspects of the Cold War. Failure to husband financial strength led directly to the severe financial dislocations and Cold War reversals of the 1970s and the massive deficits the nation still bears."[155]

President Eisenhower used his experience as a military leader to deal with the problems he faced when he came into office. He believed in care staff work. Eisenhower preferred an organized chain of command that could quickly gather and analyze data and prepare responses for action. "Ike" established administrative procedures for policy making and response that were based on:[156]

Uncovering facts, careful examination to determine the truth.

Options that were coordinated and approved by interested agencies with disagreements highlighted and not compromised.

Analysists ready to debate both sides of an issue in the presence of the President.

A final statement of the President's decision to avoid uncertainty and ambiguity.

President Truman created the National Security Council (NSC) in 1947 with the intent to insure coordination among the military forces and the Central Intelligence Agency (CIA). Truman believed that the State Department alone and diplomacy could not effectively deal with the Soviet threat. Under Ike, the NSC evolved into the main arm of the President to implement international, military and internal security policies. Eisenhower used the NSC extensively as his principle instrument to govern in a rapidly changing world that required immediate responses. The Council consisted of the President, Vice President, Secretaries of State and Defense and the Director of Office of Defense Mobilization. A score of other

---

[155] Aaron Lobel, Editor, Presidential Judgment, Futurecasts online magazine, www.futurecasts.com, Volume 5, No. 1,1/03
[156] Ibid Lobel

Cabinet members and senior advisers could be called upon depending on the question being dealt with. The Secretary of the Treasury and the Chairman of the Joint Chiefs of Staff often participated. The Director of Central Intelligence provided regular briefings on global occurrences affecting national security.

The President gave special emphasis to the NSC meetings. He attended 173 of the 179 meeting during his first term. He missed six due to travel. "At NSC meetings, Ike would actively question, comment, and sometimes play devil's advocate, to explore alternatives or the consequences or implications of some proposal. This system succeeded in producing active discussions and debates on contentious issues. Competing analyses and debate succeeded in facilitating informed and sound decisions."[157] A major part of the NSC was the Planning Board. It consisted of top notch analysists who prepared policy reports that were reviewed at the meetings. The Board was responsible for creating "statesman-like-solutions" to thorny security problems. The Board was required to present candid views and not search for compromises among the agencies. Ike's approach to problem-solving and handling the unexpected was effective in keeping foreign crises from turning into military conflicts. It laid down a well-organized procedure for emergency preparedness and reduced risks in Presidential decision making. Ike cited several accomplishments as he left the White House in 1960:

The Interstate Highway system and the St. Lawrence Seaway

Civil Rights Bill of 1957

Balance of the Federal Budget

End of the Korean War

Eight years of Peace and Economic Growth

The Eisenhower approach was abandoned by John Kennedy and subsequent administrations. The form of the NSC was maintained

---

[157] Ibid Lobel

but the substance of decision making shifted to a handful of advisers, in most cases. The Assistant to the President for National Security became the key policy adviser to the Chief Executive. The staff was large and seemed like a mini Department of State. The Planning Board was eliminated. As a result, Presidential decisions became more "ad hoc" at the expense of long term coherence and common sense.For example, the Bay of Pigs debacle may not have occurred if President Kennedy had used the NSC approach to analyze the details of the operation and anticipate the consequences of his decisions. [158]

LBJ's Great society by Lloyd Ostendorf, Courtesy American Gallery—20th century

Lyndon Johnson used a more personal approach to dealing with foreign policy and national security issues, often relying on his own

---

[158] Ibid Lobel

instincts and experience in making judgments. He did not like large NSC meetings supported by extensive staff work. He, like Kennedy, was afraid of "leaks" of information reaching the media. Cabinet officers, like Dean Rusk and Robert McNamara were reluctant to participate in sessions with large gatherings where extensive discussions were the norm and the chance that comments could reach the press were possible.

Richard Nixon relied on Henry Kissinger, his National Security Advisor to plan and direct foreign policy from the Oval Office. The NSC under Kissinger was shaped to meet his needs and those of the President. The close relationship between Nixon and Kissinger resulted in America undertaking dramatic foreign policy initiatives like the opening up to China. It resulted in an increase in power for Kissinger, more frequent consultations with the President and unchallenged authority of the NSC. Gerald Ford kept Kissinger on when he took over from Nixon.

Jimmy Carter felt that the Kissinger/Nixon style of foreign policy was dangerous. He instead relied on his cabinet and left the NSC to be a policy arm of the Executive Branch. A return to a more extensive use of the NSC came about during the administration of George H.W. Bush. He created a series of policy coordinating committees that analyzed decisions for the President in an organized manner. The new NSC stressed cooperation among the agencies and clear decision making options for the President. The Bush changes were the closest to those originally put into place by Eisenhower.

Bill Clinton abolished the Bush procedure. He preferred a Presidential Decision Directive to promulgate executive decisions. He added a broad economic element to the work of the NSC. George W. Bush depended more on the Nixon/Kissinger model with Condoleezza Rice as National Security Assistant bolstered by Secretary of State Colin Powell and Donald Rumsfeld at Defense.

Like his immediate predecessors, President Obama uses a small group of advisers to deal with foreign policy issues vs the NSC process which can be detailed and cumbersome.[159]

The next President should be measured by how they plan to face administratively the huge problems that are simultaneously happening around the world: economic decline, environmental challenges, terrorism, pandemics and issues of war and peace. Some thoughts to handle rapidly changing events for:[160]

Not everything is controllable.

Actions may have to be taken without complete knowledge even though every effort must be made to make decisions based on facts. Build a team of thinkers who anticipate the best and worst scenarios *before* they happen.

Some choices will be wrong. It may be better than no decision.

Avoid decisions based on pride. If a bad decision was made, take responsibility and make a new one.

Be prepared for the unexpected.

Plans need to be revisited and updated regularly.

Show confidence by making thoughtful decisions and sticking to them; listen carefully to everyone, even the critics; be humble and avoid notoriety even if you are President; most of all be willing to give others credit when you succeed and take the blame when you fail. This stimulates strong moral and loyalty and promotes innovation.

---

[159] Karen DeYoung, How the Obama Administration Runs Foreign Policy, The Washington Post, August 4th, 2009

[160] Shaw Dealing with Ambiguity: The New Business Imperative, Aug 29, 2013https://www.linkedin.com/pulse/20130829124922-284615-dealing-with-ambiguity-the-new-business-imperative

Listen to your inner voice and intuition in making final decisions. You may not always be right but you may not always be wrong.

Surround yourself with the best and the brightest and listen to them. Search for "contrarian views" and study them. Do not steal other's ideas and give attribution.

Mange stress. The uncertainty in the world will overcome a President who does not cultivate and maintain a relaxed state of mind. Leadership is lonely. It requires mental and physical balance to maintain stability. Lincoln relaxed by telling stories. At times, they were to make a point but more often, they allowed him to take his mind off the tragedies that encircled his daily life. He had a good sense of humor. Illustrious leaders often do not take themselves seriously and are able to use humor to teach as well as reduce tension. Responsibility results in high stress. It demands energy, careful pacing of work and monitoring good health. Mental and physical health is essential, if a President is to tackle the obligations that come with command.[161]

Abraham Lincoln created the National Academy of Sciences in 1863. Since then, the scientific community has devoted itself to research and understanding the shape of things to come. Professor James Martin of Oxford University Institute for Science and Civilization, wrote *"The Meaning of the 21st Century; A Vital Blueprint for Ensuring Our Future."*

In his study he outlined those developments that will be part of the agenda dealing with change of the new President of the United States in 2016:

Saving the Earth

Reversing Poverty

Steadying Population Growth

Achieving Sustainable Lifestyles

---

[161] Ibid Iodice, p. 282

Preventing All-Out War

Dealing Effectively with Globalism

Protecting the Biosphere

Defusing Terrorism

Conquering Disease

Expanding Human Potential

To improve is to change; to be perfect is to change often. Winston Churchill

Chapter Thirteen: Loves Learning

It's what you learn after you know it all that counts. **John Wooden**

Live as if you were to die tomorrow. Learn as if you were to live forever. **Mahatma Gandhi**

Education is what remains after one has forgotten what one has learned in school. **Albert Einstein**

I am not afraid of storms for I am learning how to sail my ship. **Louisa May Alcott**

I like to listen. I have learned a great deal from listening carefully. Most people never listen. **Ernest Hemingway**

You cannot open a book without learning something. **Confucius**

Being ignorant is not so much a shame, as being unwilling to learn. **Benjamin Franklin**

We now accept the fact that learning is a lifelong process of keeping abreast of change. And the most pressing task is to teach people how to learn. **Peter Drucker**

A single conversation across the table with a wise man is better than ten years mere study of books. **Henry Wadsworth Longfellow**

In this life, you should read everything you can read. Taste everything you can taste. Meet everyone you can meet. Travel everywhere you can travel. Learn everything you can learn. Experience everything you can experience. **Mario Cuomo**

Learning is a key pillar of Presidential leadership. Information is fast paced and needs to be refreshed constantly. Talented leaders want facts, love knowledge, are curious about novelty and innovation and appreciate that learning is a lifelong experience. Great leaders learn from their peers. They meet and converse with others who are facing similar challenges.[162] They learn about new ideas and innovations.

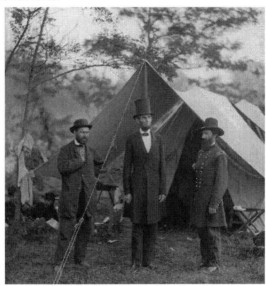

Lincoln at Antietam, Courtesy Library of Congress

Abraham Lincoln: Technology and Shakespeare

Abraham Lincoln, for instance, was fascinated with new technology. In the White House, Lincoln believed he was

---

[162] Ibid Iodice

competent to handle challenges related to technology. As a surveyor and patent lawyer he became skilled at how to study innovations. Lincoln realized his inadequacies because of a lack of formal education but this did not prevent him from being eternally curious especially about the latest inventions that could change the outcome of the Civil War. Any new fire arm, for example, was of interest to him. He disliked hunting but was still proficient with a rifle and participated in marksmanship contests when visiting soldiers on the battlefield. Inventors of all sorts of weapons would descend on the White House to exhibit their "working models" to the President. If he was interested, he would turn it over to the professionals in the military to examine their feasibility. [163] In addition to being interested in innovation, Lincoln read extensively.

Lincoln loved Shakespeare and recited passages from plays. During a White House dinner with an actor as a guest, Lincoln said, "Some of Shakespeare's plays I have never read; while others I have gone over perhaps as frequently as any unprofessional reader. Among the latter are *Lear*, *Richard the Third*, *Henry the Eighth*, *Hamlet*, and especially *Macbeth*. I think nothing equals *Macbeth*." [164] He enjoyed music and went to the theatre as frequently as he could. It was a way to relax from the rigors of his office.

Lincoln adored reading poetry. He memorized his favorite verses and recited them. Lincoln wrote several sonnets based on childhood memories. In the White House he received from 50 to 250 letters a day, some included poems. He read them with pleasure

[163] Robert Bruce, Lincoln and the Tools of War, University of Illinois Press, Springfield, 1989.p 14.

[164] David Odegard, The Favorite Books of All 44 Presidents of the United States, Feb. 17, 2014, http://www.buzzfeed.com/daveodegard/the-favorite-books-of-all-44-presidents-of-the-united-states#.wbpn9bdpn

and saved some of them.[165] Poetry influenced his speaking and writing, which he felt was the greatest idea man had ever created.

Writing, the art of communicating thoughts to the mind, through the eye—is the great invention of the world. Great in the astonishing range of analysis and combination . . . great in enabling us to converse with the dead, the absent, and the unborn, at all distances of time and space. **Abraham Lincoln**

WORLD WAR II ALLIES - Russia's Joseph Stalin, FDR and Winston Churchill of Great Britain meet in Teheran, Iran, Nov. 29, 1943. Courtesy: Roosevelt Library

FDR: Avid Reader and Collector

Franklin Roosevelt was an avid reader and had an enormous interest in so many subjects. His favorite authors were Kipling, Dickens and

Twain. He also read contemporary subjects especially those related to history. He collected books, models of ships and memorabilia of all sorts. Scarcely a day would go by that FDR did not work on his stamp collection while in the White House. He found it linked him to history and geography around the world. His collection at his death was over 1,200,000 stamps. Those he received from foreign governments were donated to the Franklin Delano Roosevelt Presidential Library at Hyde Park. He also gave to the Library 200 fully rigged ship models, 1,200 naval prints and 15,000 books, thousands of pages of newspaper clippings, articles, speeches, letters, memos and countless souvenirs of all sorts. FDR realized that to house his collection he would have to establish the first Presidential library. He had the public interest in mind. He wanted to create an historical research institution to educate the people about his time in office. On June 30th, 1941, FDR opened the library with these words: [166]

The dedication of a library is in itself an act of faith. To bring together the records of the past and to house them in buildings where they will be preserved for the use of men and women in the future, a Nation must believe in three things. It must believe in the past. It must believe in the future. It must, above all, believe in the capacity of its own people so to learn from the past that they can gain in judgment in creating their own future.

Much can be learned about a President or a candidate by what they read. Each of our Presidents enjoyed reading before and during their time in the White House. What they read often showed what their priorities were and how they saw themselves as leaders which may have affected the way they governed. Some books, in particular, influenced their thinking and future policies.

Harry Truman read extensively about Andrew Jackson. He likened himself to "Old Hickory" in his plain origins, direct style of

---

[166]Prologue Magazine, National Archives, Roosevelt and His Library, by Cynthia M. Koch and Lynn A. Bassanese, Summer 2001, Vol 33, No. 2

speaking and governing. [167]   A book review influenced John Kennedy to launch a major policy initiative of his administration. After reading about Michael Harrington's "The Other America," which was about poverty, he asked his staff to look into the issue and come and come up with an "attack on poverty." This was shortly before his trip to Dallas, in November, 1963. [168]   Barbara Ward's, "The Rich Nations and the Poor Nations," influenced Lyndon Johnson, Kennedy's successor.   He read the British author's book several times. It inspired him to move ahead with the War on Poverty, and realize Kennedy's vision.

Richard Nixon was an avid reader of Tolstoy. He also read books about the major issues of the day. After meeting with the Soviets, for example, he read Churchill's "Triumph and Tragedy" that chronicled Churchill's experience at the Yalta Conference in 1945.

Edmund Morris' books on Theodore Roosevelt were among Ronald Reagan's favorites.   Morris, in fact, became Reagan's official biographer.   "The Gipper," was the first President to highlight works of conservative economists and intellectuals like "Free to Choose," by Milton Friedman and George Gilder's "Wealth and Poverty."[169]

Ralph Ellison, Maya Angelou and Taylor Branch were among Bill Clinton's favorite writers. He loved mysteries. He often stressed books of thinkers like Yale law professor Stephen Carter by displaying them prominently in the Oval Office. "The Balkan Ghosts" by Robert Kaplan apparently influenced Clinton's decision to intervene in Bosnia. During his second term, George W. Bush

---

[167] Jon Meacham, How to Read Like a President, New York Times Essay, October 31st, 2008, http://www.nytimes.com/2008/11/02/books/review/Meacham-t.html?_r=0

[168] Tevi Troy, For Obama and past presidents, the books they read shape policies and perceptions, The Washington Post, Sunday, April 18th, 2010

[169] Ibid Troy

read extensively. He liked what were described as "prescriptive books" like "Supreme Command" by Eliot A. Cohen and "The Case for Democracy," by Natan Sharansky. These advocated military and nation building policies. Bush met with authors whose books he enjoyed. Sharansky, for example, spent an hour with him in the Oval Office discussing how to advance democracy in the world. "Not only did he read it," said Sharansky," he felt it. [170]

America will need a President who loves learning in 2016. We need a program comparable to landing a man on the moon to revitalize our educational system especially at the elementary level. Tony Wagner, in his book, The Global Achievement Gap outlined what is essential for learning in the 21st Century:

Critical Thinking and Problem Solving

Collaboration across Networks and Leading by Influence

Agility and Adaptability

Initiative and Entrepreneurialism

Effective Oral and Written Communication

Accessing and Analyzing Information

Curiosity and Imagination

The next President will have to develop a program to deal with these skills that need to be taught to our children for them to survive in the future.

---

[170] Ibid Troy

Chapter 14: Respects Diversity

Tolerance implies no lack of commitment to one's own beliefs. Rather it condemns the oppression or persecution of others.
John F. Kennedy

What is tolerance? It is the consequence of humanity. We are all formed of frailty and error; let us pardon reciprocally each other's folly - that is the first law of nature. **Voltaire**

The highest result of education is tolerance. **Helen Keller**

Tolerance is giving to every other human being every right that you claim for yourself. **Robert Gree**

The responsibility of tolerance lies with those who have the wider vision. **George Eliott**

It's not how much or how little you have that makes you great or small, but how much or how little you are with what you have.
Rabbi Samson Raphael Hirsch

Intolerance lies at the core of evil.
Not the intolerance that results
from any threat or danger.
But intolerance of another being who dares to exist.
Intolerance without cause. It is so deep within us,
because every human being secretly desires
the entire universe to himself.
Our only way out is to learn
compassion without cause. To care for each other
simple because that 'other' exists. **Rabbi Menachem Mendle**

Lincoln and the Jews

The United States is one of the most diverse cultures in the world. Every race, creed and color is in America. Our strength is our diversity. Our President must see it this way. Our power as a people is the respect for our differences. It was not always as such, especially when we recall our experience with slavery, the rights of women, religious discrimination and the intolerance toward those not like ourselves. Immigrants, in particular, faced this challenge from the beginnings of our republic. One of our Presidents was the glowing example of how *we should be* and how every President should be when it comes to treating other human beings. He followed the golden rule. He was tolerant, understanding of the rights of minorities and those without the power to defend themselves. He lived his life like he preached it and professed it. His name was Abraham Lincoln.

The last posed photograph of Abraham Lincoln, taken ten weeks before his assassination.
Alexander Gardner, Library of Congress

We know so much about him and his hatred of slavery and the plight of African Americans but there is another example that today gives us an additional dimension to Lincoln that we did not know before.

His relationship with Jews was an illustration of his good heart, his sense of fairness and his desire to allow all Americans a chance to live peacefully in their chosen land without the heavy hand of prejudice oppressing them.[171]

From his earliest days in Kentucky and Illinois, Lincoln came in contact with Jews. One of his closest associates and friends was Abraham Jonas. He was a lawyer, born in England, who had come to the US in 1819. Jonas and Lincoln were supporters of Henry Clay and the Whigs. Jonas helped organize the Lincoln and Douglas debates and worked to help him become President. Lincoln made him a postmaster in Quincy, Illinois. Shortly after Jonas' death, Lincoln appointed his widow to the post so as not to leave the family without a livelihood. Lincoln was close to Jonas' children. Five moved to the South. Two joined the Confederate cause. Even so, Lincoln's relationship with them was considerate and compassionate. One of Jonas's sons, an attorney, asked Lincoln in 1857 to help release a black man imprisoned in New Orleans because he lacked papers. Lincoln moved swiftly. He secured the money to save the man. In the middle of the Civil War, Lincoln's friend, Abraham Jonas was dying. The President allowed one of Jonas' sons, a Confederate prisoner of war, a parole to see his father before he died.

The Jonas friendship is only one example of Lincoln's respect and admiration for the Jews. More important, Lincoln wanted to promote a sense of fairness toward them and other minorities. He arranged for Jews to be appointed to positions in the War effort. He overturned an edict from his most popular General, Ulysses S.

---

[171] The Unusual Relationship Among Abraham Lincoln and the Jews, http://mosaicmagazine.com/observation/2015/04/the-unusual-relationship-between-abraham-lincoln-and-the-jews/

Grant, expelling Jewish merchants who were suspected of selling contraband. Lincoln would not accept such a verdict which was clearly without merit. Abraham Lincoln ran counter-current to the thinking of his day. His approach to the Jews is a case point of his broadmindedness and acceptance of all those who faced subjugation and persecution and who were misjudged and mistreated because they were in the minority. His magnificent qualities of kindness, empathy and open-mindedness were demonstrated through actions during his life and during his time as Chief Executive of the United States. Lincoln showed us what a President of the United States must have to be the leader of not just some of the people but all of the people.

Woodrow Wilson and African Americans

Woodrow Wilson, 1913, Courtesy Library of Congress

"Segregation is not humiliating but a benefit, and ought to be so regarded by you gentlemen." **Woodrow Wilson**
Source: Conference with members of the National Association for Equal Rights (November 1914), defending the re-segregation of federal offices.

The white people of the country, as well as I, wish to see the colored people progress, and admire the progress they have already made, and want to see them continue along independent lines. There is, however, a great prejudice against colored people. . . . It will take one hundred years to eradicate this prejudice, and we must deal with it as practical men. Segregation is not humiliating, but a benefit, and ought to be so regarded by you gentlemen. If your organization goes out and tells the colored people of the country that it is a humiliation, they will so regard it, but if you do not tell them so, and regard it rather as a benefit, they will regard it the same. The only harm that will come will be if you cause them to think it is a humiliation. **Woodrow Wilson**

Source: *The Crisis,* January, 1915, 119–20. Reprinted in William Loren Katz, *Eyewitness: The Negro in American History* (New York: Pitman Publishing Corporation, 1967), 389–90.

A President is able to reverse the course of events in many ways. One of which is how he manages the Executive Branch of the Federal Government. A century ago, this was especially so. The President still had considerable power over the bureaucracy despite laws promoting a meritocracy. An example is Woodrow Wilson. He was the first Southerner to be elected to the Oval Office since the Civil War. His legacy has been that of a liberal progressive who fought for humanitarian rights and social justice at home and abroad.

One hundred years after Wilson assumed the Presidency, articles came out in the New York Times and elsewhere questioning his position among those of great Presidents. The issue was Wilson's actions against African Americans which swept away much of the progress they achieved as public servants since the end of the Civil War. Theodore Roosevelt and William Howard Taft worked to open the federal government to people of all races. Roosevelt's reforms of the Civil Service, in particular, were designed to reduce the effect of the "spoils system" and create a merit based process of hiring.

The Editorial Board of the New York Times wrote about this on November 24th, 1915 in an article entitled, *The Case Against Woodrow Wilson at Princeton:*

"Wilson, who took office in 1913, inherited a federal government that had been shaped during the late 19th and early 20th centuries, when thousands of African-American men and women passed Civil Service examinations or received political appointments that landed them in well-paying, middle-class government jobs in which they sometimes supervised white workers. This was anathema to Wilson, who believed that black Americans were unworthy of full citizenship and admired the Ku Klux Klan for the role it had in terrorizing African-Americans to restrict their political power."

Woodrow Wilson's Cabinet, 1913, Courtesy Library of Congress

Historian Eric Yellin, in his book "Racism in the Nation's Service, Government Workers and Color Line in Woodrow Wilson's America," (University of North Carolina Press, 2013), notes that Wilson appointed segregationists to his Cabinet who shared his views about African Americans. Among them was William McAdoo as Secretary of the Treasury and Albert Burleson as Postmaster General. Both officials set about segregating their departments and firing or demoting blacks. Wilson had tried to appoint an African American to the position of Register of the Treasury but withdrew the nomination after the protest of Democratic Senators from the South.

The New York Times's Editorial Board ended their case against Wilson with this story:

"For John Abraham Davis, a black midlevel manager in the Government Printing Office with 30 years' experience, the change came almost overnight. Just months after Wilson was sworn in, Davis was demoted to a succession of menial jobs and ended up as a messenger making half his original salary. As his grandson, Gordon Davis, wrote on the Op-Ed page on Tuesday: 'By April 1914, the family farm was auctioned off. John Davis, a self-made black man of achievement and stature in his community at the turn of the 20th century, was, by the end of Wilson's first term, a broken man. He died in 1928.'"

The impact of his actions reverberated for decades after he left office. The policy established by the Wilson Administration against blacks became the norm of federal discrimination which lasted deep into the 20th century.

Chapter 15: Trust

It takes 20 years to build a reputation and five minutes to ruin it. **Warren Buffett**

Whoever is careless with the truth in small matters cannot be trusted with important matters. **Albert Einstein**

I have no fear that the result of our experiment will be that men may be trusted to govern themselves without a master. **Thomas Jefferson**

Trust, but verify. **Ronald Reagan**

Responsibilities are given to him on whom trust rests. Responsibility is always a sign of trust. **James Cash Penne**

He who does not trust enough, will not be trusted. **Lao Tzu**

I cannot trust a man to control others who cannot control himself. **Robert E. Lee**

Trust has to be earned, and should come only after the passage of time. **Arthur Ashe**

Few things can help an individual more than to place responsibility on him, and to let him know that you trust him. **B. T. Washington**

Government is a trust, and the officers of the government are trustees. And both the trust and the trustees are created for the benefit of the people. **Henry Clay**

The Vietnam War

Vietnam: Confusing, oxymoronic, lethal, torrential, steaming, wasteful...They came home without leaving Vietnam, angry and depressed, retreating from the world and burdened by memories of the dead... the war taught a generation of young people not to trust their government. Stars and Stripes

Vietnam Memorial, Washington, DC, Courtesy National Archives

By the time US military involvement in Vietnam ended in August, 1975, 282,000 Allied military personnel had died. 58,220 were Americans. 444,000 North Vietnamese and Viet Cong lost their lives along with 587,000 North and South Vietnamese civilians. 1,313,000 people died in the War in Vietnam. Nearly 3 million Americans served in Vietnam...10% of their generation.[172]

Americans fought bravely. They won nearly every battle and were awarded 250 Medals of Honor. It was all in vain. "They, and so many others who fought in Vietnam, were as great as any

---

[172] Lewy, Guenter (1978), *America in Vietnam*, New York: Oxford University Press, pp. 442–453

generation that preceded them. Their misfortune was to draw a bad war, an unnecessary war, a mistake by American politicians and statesmen, for which they paid."[173]

Many returned home disillusioned with the government that sent them to fight in a far off jungle for a questionable cause. Millions of Americans protested against the War across the United States for nearly a decade. Americans and many of their leaders lost faith in their government. "The biggest lesson I learned from Vietnam is not to trust our own government statements. I had no idea until then that you could not rely on them," former Sen. J. William Fulbright.[174]

Hundreds of thousands of bombs and tens of thousands of gallons of Agent Orange were dropped on Vietnam. Forty years after the end of the War, the Vietnamese are still cleaning up the land ravaged by one of the fiercest bombing campaigns in history. The US government is paying for part of the effort. [175] What can never be repaid is the human suffering caused by the War and loss of faith in our political system and way of life. Vietnam was caused by Presidential leadership and Presidential decisions that were wrong and lies and mistruths that created a lasting sense of mistrust toward our system of government that prevails to the present day.

---

[173] Neil Sheehan, At the Bloody Dawn of the Vietnam War, The New York Times, November 13th, 2015

[174] By Terry Leonard, Vietnam at 50, Stars and Stripes, 2015, http://www.stripes.com/news/special-reports/vietnam-at-50

[175] George Black, The Lethal Legacy of the Vietnam War, Fifty years after the first US troops came ashore at Da Nang, the Vietnamese are still coping with unexploded bombs and Agent Orange. The Nation, February 25, 2015 http://www.thenation.com/article/lethal-legacy-vietnam-war/

Secretary of Defense, Robert McNamara served John Kennedy and Lyndon Johnson. He was a chief architect of the War. In his book, Retrospect: the Tragedy and Lessons of Vietnam, he said:[176]

Although we sought to do the right thing - and believed we were doing the right thing - in my judgment, hindsight proves us wrong. We both overestimated the effects of South Vietnam's loss on the security of the West and failed to adhere to the fundamental principle that, in the final analysis, if the South Vietnamese were to be saved, they had to win the war themselves.

Presidential Historian, Doris Kearns Goodwin commented on the legacy of the War and Presidential leadership:[177]

... the most important lesson that people have to take from the war... is that no foreign war can succeed without that large domestic support. Franklin Roosevelt understood that way back in the 30's when he "quarantine the aggressor speech," and the country didn't respond to want to go get involved in Europe's war. Later he said it's like looking back in a parade and no one's following you. You can't go forward. So wherever we lay blame or not, I think there's no question that the lesson to be learned is you have to level with the country, you have to make them understand the price they're paying.

While the Vietnam War was continuing during Richard Nixon's second term another incident happened that shook the trust of the American people in their government and, in particular, the Presidency: Watergate.

The Watergate Scandal

The impact is deep and will be enduring. It will be a long time, if ever, before politics in the United States is the same again. **US News and World Report, August 8th, 2014**

---

[176] Legacy of the Vietnam War, http://www.footprinttravelguides.com/asia/vietnam/about-vietnam/legacy-of-the-vietnam-war/, Retrospect, The Tragedy of the Vietnam War, Robert McNamara, Vintage Books, New York, March, 1998.

[177] Doris Keans Goodwin, PBS News hour Vietnam's Legacy, April 5th, 2000, http://www.pbs.org/newshour/bb/asia-jan-june00-vietnam_4-5/TOPICS > Nation

Senate Watergate Committee holding a press conference, Courtesy US Senate Historical Office

After Gerald Ford pardoned Richard Nixon in September, 1974, Nixon expressed regret and released this statement: [178]

I was wrong in not acting more decisively and more forthrightly in dealing with Watergate, particularly when it reached the stage of judicial proceedings and grew from a political scandal into a national tragedy. No words can describe the depth of my regret and pain at the anguish my mistakes over Watergate have caused the nation and the presidency, a nation I so deeply love, and an institution I so greatly respect.

Watergate overshadowed the Nixon Presidency. Many Americans remember him as the first President to resign from office and not his achievements. The affair left such a lasting impression around the world that many scandals since then have been labeled with the suffix, "gate."

The scandal resulted in a chain reaction of measures to reign in Presidential power. A series of laws were passed reducing the President's ability to wage undeclared war, strengthening public access to government information and curbs on campaign spending. The Freedom of Information Act was amended. New financial disclosure policies went into effect for top government officials.

[178] Boundless. "The Effects of Watergate." *Boundless U.S. History*. Boundless, 21 Jul. 2015. Retrieved 13 Oct. 2015 from https://www.boundless.com/u-s-history/textbooks/boundless-u-s-history-textbook/the-conservative-turn-of-america-1968-1989.

The incident proved that the Constitutional system of checks and balances worked.

1974 Political Cartoon depicting Watergate's damage to the Presidency, Courtesy National Archives

By far the most significant impact was the public's loss of trust in the Presidency, elected officials, politicians and government in general.   Cynicism and skepticism concerning the character, honesty and motives of elected officials would be broad, deep and long lasting.[179]

---

[179] Ibid Boundless.

Karl Hubenthal, 1975, Courtesy Ohio State University Cartoon Research Library

The political fallout for the Republicans was almost immediate. Democrats made significant gains in the 1974 midterm elections and took the White House in 1976. Forty years after Vietnam and Watergate, Americans still are skeptical about the government.

A June, 2015 Pew Research Report found that Americans confidence and trust in all three branches of the government remains low. President Obama's ratings reached 33% vs 29% last year which is 4% above the 25% record low of 2007 during the Presidency of George W. Bush.

The next President and the next Congress will need to work to restore public confidence. An example of a President who was able to capture and maintain the trust of the people was Franklin Delano Roosevelt. He did it by taking action, communicating and staying close to the people and their institutions. He made it a point to reach into the households of ordinary Americans and speak to them, calm their fears and give them hope. It was this hope that ultimately carried the nation through hard times and helped us win the War.

President Franklin D. Roosevelt received an average of 8,000 letters, cards and telegrams daily.
Courtesy Franklin D. Roosevelt Presidential Library

FDR: Gaining the Public Trust

Franklin Roosevelt used the radio, the media and the pen to talk with the people. He received letters throughout his Presidency and responded personally when possible. His Fireside Chats generated an unprecedented tide of mail. On average, a broadcast would generate 450,000 letters, telegrams and cards. Herbert Hoover, FDR's predecessor received about 800 letters a day. Roosevelt received more than 8000. What follows are a few letters, from the Franklin D. Roosevelt Presidential Library that he received that show the impact he had on the public: [180]

OCTOBER 1, 1934

Dear Mr. President,

Everybody who has any sense and was able to get to a radio heard your speech last night. I desire to add my firm approval to every utterance which came from your lips.

Surely under the guidance of your great constructive genius the country is gaining. It is well that you take us into your confidence and tell us Mr. President; your address reveals what we had not heard. There is such a welter of publicity about the alphabetized programs that much wisdom is lost in confusion, but when you speak everybody understands.

You know what your government is doing. You know how to explain it. You know where you are heading and you are on your way.

God bless and keep you strong for the battle Mr. President is the sincere wish of a red-hot, jet-black Democrat.

Melvin J. Chisum
(Field Secretary of the National Negro Press Association)
Philadelphia, Pa.

APRIL 28, 1942

Dear Frank:

And I use this salutation respectfully, warmly. For any man who could come so close to people of the U.S. as you did tonight, certainly knows them well enough to be called by his first name.

This is from a 26 1/2 year old chemical engineer who would almost rather die than write a letter…

Frank, tonight you made me proud of being an American and you made me want to write, made the urge to do so irresistible…

Frank, there is one thrill, one sublime thrill that you will never know, or, rather, experience. And that is the thrill that comes to a person – who, having been brought up in a poor family, experienced and felt keenly many of the injustices in our system – when he hears one of our leaders, – – who has every justifiable right and reason, judging from his background, to be perfectly unaware of these inequalities – dedicate himself and rededicate the nation to the sublime principles of true democracy.

You see, Frank, there were times when my heard was heavy and filled with doubts times such as the miserable shooting on the bonus army, or times, when as a relief investigator I visited hundreds of downtrodden and almost hopeless families, or events such as the Republic Steel massacre in Chicago, – and I wondered whether democracy would ever rise above such low levels.

Tonight, you reaffirmed my faith and reawakened in me, that which I thought was no longer there, namely, a feeling a being one of a large, united family, and a hope that this family, – Christian and

[180] American Radio Works, Letters to Franklin Delano Roosevelt November 10, 2014
http://www.americanradioworks.org/segments/letters-to-franklin-delano-roosevelt/

Web Sites to Compare Presidential Candidates Position on Issues

In the coming weeks there will be comparisons of what the candidates believe and propose on a variety of issues. The following are a few useful web sites to consult:

http://www.nytimes.com/interactive/2015/06/04/us/politics/stacking-up-the-presidential-fields.html?_r=0

http://www.pbs.org/newshour/tag/what-the-candidates-believe/

http://www.theatlantic.com/politics/archive/2015/11/2016-election/384828/

http://nymag.com/daily/intelligencer/2014/12/guide-2016-candidates.html#

http://www.cfr.org/elections/presidential-candidates-their-own-words/p36633?cid=ppc-Google-grant-C2016_Own_Words_Gen-070915&gclid=CjwKEAiAmeyxBRCJxoKk7IWLl2oSJABvZjhh1kqVWjfVsttjmYfBodFV3mm80rlCLzxmKBi8WGHOjBoCTf7w_wcB

Bibliography

Lincoln Biographies

Beveridge, Albert J. *Abraham Lincoln: 1809-1858* (1928). 2 vol. to 1858; online edition

Burlingame, Michael. *Abraham Lincoln: A Life* (2 vol 2008).

Carwardine, Richard. *Lincoln: A Life of Purpose and Power* (2003)

Cuomo, Mario, Why Lincoln Matters, Harcourt, New York, 2004

DeRose, Chris *Congressman Lincoln: The Making of America's Greatest President* (2013). http://www.amazon.com/Congressman-Lincoln-Chris-DeRose/dp/1451695144

Gienapp, William E. *Abraham Lincoln and Civil War America: A Biography* (2002), online edition

Goodwin, Doris Kearns. *Team of Rivals: The Political Genius of Abraham Lincoln* (2005.

Guelzo, Allen C. *Abraham Lincoln: Redeemer President* (1999) online edition

Harris, William C. *Lincoln's Rise to the Presidency* (2007) Nicolay, John George and John Hay. *Abraham Lincoln: a History* (1890); online at Volume 1 and Volume 2 vol 6 10 volumes in all.

Neely, Mark E. *The Last Best Hope of Earth: Abraham Lincoln and the Promise of America* (1993).

Oates, Stephen B. *With Malice Toward None: The Life of Abraham Lincoln* (1994) excerpt and text search

Sandburg, Carl. *Abraham Lincoln: The Prairie Years* (2 vol 1926); *The War Years* (4 vol 1939). vol. 1 online vol 2 online

Thomas, Benjamin P. *Abraham Lincoln: A Biography* (1952; 2nd ed. 2008) online edition

White, Ronald C. Jr., A. Lincoln: A Biography, Random House, New York, 2009

White, Ronald C. Jr., The Eloquent President, Random House, 2005

White, Ronald C. Jr., Lincoln's Greatest Speech, Simon and Shuster, New York, 2002

Presidential Biographies

Bumiller, Elisabeth (January 2009). "Inside the Presidency". National Geographic 2015 (1): 130–149.

 Beschloss, Michael, Presidential Courage: Brave Leaders and How They Changed America 1789-1989, by Michael Beschloss, Simon & Schuster, May 200

Couch, Ernie. Presidential Trivia. Rutledge Hill Press. March 1, 1996. Lang, J. Stephen. The Complete Book of Presidential Trivia. Pelican Publishing. 2001.

Leo, Leonard – Taranto, James – Bennett, William J. Presidential Leadership: Rating the Best and the Worst in the White House. Simon and Schuster. 2004.

Presidential Studies Quarterly, published by Blackwell Synergy, is a quarterly academic journal on the presidency.

Waldman, Michael – Stephanopoulos, George. My Fellow Americans: The Most Important Speeches of America's Presidents, from George Washington to George W. Bush. Sourcebooks Trade. 2003. ISBN 1-4022-0027-7

Winder, Michael K. Presidents and Prophets: The Story of America's Presidents and the LDS Church. Covenant Communications. 2007.

Presidential Histories

Jacobs, Ron. Interview with Joseph G. Peschek and William Grover, authors of The Unsustainable Presidency.

A New Nation Votes: American Election Returns, 1787–1825
Presidential election returns including town and county
breakdowns

*"The American Presidency Project". UC Santa Barbara. Retrieved
October 7, 2005.* Collection of over 67,000 presidential
documents

The History Channel: US Presidents

*"All the President's Roles". Ask Gleaves. Retrieved October 20,
2006.* Hauenstein Center for Presidential Studies Educational site
on the American presidency

"Presidents' Occupations". Retrieved August 20, 2007.

"The Presidents". American Experience. Retrieved March 4, 2007.
PBS site on the American presidency

Presidents of the United States: Resource Guides from the Library
of Congress

Franklin Delano Roosevelt Biographies

*Davis, Kenneth S (1972), FDR: The Beckoning of Destiny, 1882–
1928 (popular biography), ISBN 978-0-399-10998-0.*

*Freidel, Frank (1952–73), Franklin D. Roosevelt, 4 volumes,
(1990), Franklin D. Roosevelt: A Rendezvous with Destiny
(scholarly biography), one volume,* covers entire life.

*Goodwin, Doris Kearns (1995), No Ordinary Time: Franklin and
Eleanor Roosevelt: The Home Front in World War II,*

*Gunther, John (1950), Roosevelt in Retrospect, Harper &
Brothers*

*Hawley, Ellis (1995). The New Deal and the Problem of
Monopoly. Fordham University Press. ISBN 0-8232-1609-8.*

*Jenkins, Roy (2003), Franklin Delano Roosevelt (short bio from
British perspective), ISBN 978-0-8050-6959-4.*

After the Foreign Service he was named Vice President of Lucent Technologies in charge of operations in numerous countries and later taught full time a Trinity College in Washington, DC.

Today he is Vice President of a major university and a Professor of Leadership. He speaks several languages, has traveled across the globe and his passions in life are good music, writing and reading, his family and, in particular, his four grandchildren.

In 2012 his bestselling book on tenor Mario Lanza was published entitled, *"A Kid from Philadelphia, Mario Lanza: The Voice of the Poets."* In 2013 his second book, *"Profiles in Leadership from Caesar to Modern Times"* was published." In 2014 he published *"Sisters,"* the story of two extraordinary people, his mother and aunt as well as *"Future Shock 2.0, The Dragon Brief 2020"* a work of fiction based on fact looking at the future of the world. Recently he published *"Reflections, Stories of Love, Leadership, Courage and Passion."* Proceeds from sales of his books go to charitable causes. **efiodice@yahoo.com**

Index

Courtesy Mount Rushmore National Memorial

47813516R00188

Made in the USA
Lexington, KY
14 December 2015